THE FILMS OF

HEDY LAMARR

BY CHRISTOPHER YOUNG

THE CITADEL PRESS   SECAUCUS, N. J.

Also by
CHRISTOPHER YOUNG
THE FILMS OF DORIS DAY

First edition
Copyright © 1978 by
Christopher Young
All rights reserved

Published by Citadel Press
A division of Lyle Stuart Inc.
120 Enterprise Ave.
Secaucus, N. J. 07094

In Canada:
George J. McLeod Limited
Don Mills, Ont.

Manufactured in the
United States of America
by Halliday Lithograph
West Hanover, Mass.

DESIGN BY LESTER GLASSNER

Library of Congress Cataloging in Publication Data

Young, Christopher.
  The films of Hedy Lamarr.

  1. Lamarr, Hedy, 1915-   2. Moving-picture
actors and actresses—Biography.   I. Title.
PN2287.I24Y68   791.43'028'0924   78-11624
ISBN 0-8065-0579-6

To my beautiful mother
VIRGINIA OXLEY MORISON
and my wonderful grandmother
BESSIE BEAL OXLEY
with love

My thanks to

ARTHUR METZGAR, BUDDY MARSHALL AND JOHN FERREL

for their invaluable assistance and encouragement

and to

LESTER GLASSNER

for his excellent design and layout.

Grateful acknowledgment is also expressed to the following for their various contributions:

DAVID MORISON	JUNE ALLYSON	ANTHONY LODER	REX REED
TRUDE KIESLER	ALICE CARTER	POLLY WHITING	JUNE BASS
ROBERT FRIESS	ROY N. OXLEY	LOU VALENTINO	GENE BURD
KIRK CRIVELLO	NICK PASQUAL	ROSE SARGENT	ERIC BENSON
NIGEL STANNARD	PATRICK AGAN	HOMER DICKENS	GEORGE ZENO
VONALEE HUCKINS	JOHN R. COCCHI	RICHARD WHITING	GWEN GRANT
PHILIP CASTANZA	DARRELL ARROWSMITH	MYRON GOLDSTEIN	VILMA ZENO

Immeasurable help was furnished by the staffs of the following organizations: Oesterreichische Nationalbibliothek, Vienna; Det Danske Filmmuseum, Copenhagen; The Academy of Motion Picture Arts and Sciences, Beverly Hills; Lincoln Center Library of the Performing Arts, New York City; Metro-Goldwyn-Mayer, Munich and Vienna; Paramount Pictures (Bill Kenly), New York City; and The Mike Douglas Show (Mike Leshnov and Owen S. Simon), Philadelphia.

Special Thanks to

MISS HEDY LAMARR

a very lovely and gracious lady

All photographs from The Christopher Young Collection

CONTENTS

HEDY LAMARR

YOU STEPPED OUT OF A DREAM   **11**

THE TRANSCENDENT BEAUTY   **55**

THE FILMS OF HEDY LAMARR   **77**

Geld Auf Der Strasse   79

Sturm im Wasserglas   81

Wir Brauchen Kein Geld   85

Die Koffer Des Herrn O.F.   89

Ekstase   92

Algiers   99

Lady of the Tropics   106

I Take This Woman   113

Boom Town   119

Comrade X   125

Come Live With Me   128

Ziegfeld Girl   135

H.M. Pulham, Esq.   145

Tortilla Flat   151

Crossroads   157

White Cargo   162

The Heavenly Body   171

The Conspirators   175

Experiment Perilous   180

Her Highness and the Bellboy   185

The Strange Woman   188

Dishonored Lady   195

Let's Live a Little   199

Samson and Delilah   202

A Lady Without Passport   211

Copper Canyon   215

My Favorite Spy   218

Eterna Femmina   222

The Story of Mankind   227

The Female Animal   230

SHORT SUBJECTS AND FEATURE FILM CLIPS   **234**

THE LAMARR WOMEN   **236**

HEDY ON TELEVISION   **249**

HEDY LAMARR= YOU STEPPED OUT OF A DREAM

During the 1930s and 1940s, Hollywood was truly the great dream factory. From the sound stages and production lots of its studios, the directors, movie stars, and technicians who labored on this gigantic production line sent forth a series of packaged dreams that seemed endless. In those years of Depression and war, they were products we needed badly.

And on this talented production line, not one of those packagers of dreams was more beautiful or exciting than Hedy Lamarr. Hers was the beauty and excitement that once made a Paris audience gasp "Ecstasy!" and so named her most famous movie.

But after a galaxy of headaches and heartaches caused by six ill-starred marriages, the loss of a fortune, and a well-publicized arrest on a shoplifting charge, Hedy Lamarr still believes that her beauty brought on most of her troubles.

"Everywhere I find men who pay homage to my beauty and show no interest in me," she complained once.

One foolish young man even killed himself when she refused to marry him, and her first husband was so jealous of her that he locked her up in his palace.

When she arrived in the United States, Ed Sullivan wrote in his column that she was the most beautiful woman of the century. Few could dispute that assertion. When you looked at the raven hair and sensuous mouth, the upturned nose and tranquil dark eyes, you were transfixed by what you saw.

"The most beautiful girl in all Europe," Max Reinhardt, the great director and impresario, called her.

"She is conceded by most artists to be the outstanding beauty of the decade, and she is also one of the most vivacious and interesting," said famed cover photographer Paul Hesse of the Hedy Lamarr he knew at the height of her Hollywood popularity. "She is stimulating, witty, breezy, and altogether fascinating."

In *Ziegfeld Girl,* Tony Martin sang "You Stepped Out of a Dream" to her. It seems an apt description of the Viennese beauty who graced thirty European and American movies between 1930 and 1957.

From the "You Stepped Out of a Dream" number in
ZIEGFELD GIRL

Hedwig Eva Maria Kiesler at eighteen months

She was born Hedwig Eva Maria Kiesler on November 9, 1914 in Vienna, Austria. Her parents were Emil and Gertrud Kiesler. Her father was the well-to-do manager of the Kreditanstalt Bankverein, one of the leading banks in Vienna, who had come from Lemberg in the West Ukraine. Frau Kiesler was the former Gertrud Lichtwitz, born in Budapest and fifteen years younger than her husband. She had had aspirations of becoming a concert pianist but gave up the idea when her daughter was born. From that time on, all of her attention was focused on her daughter.

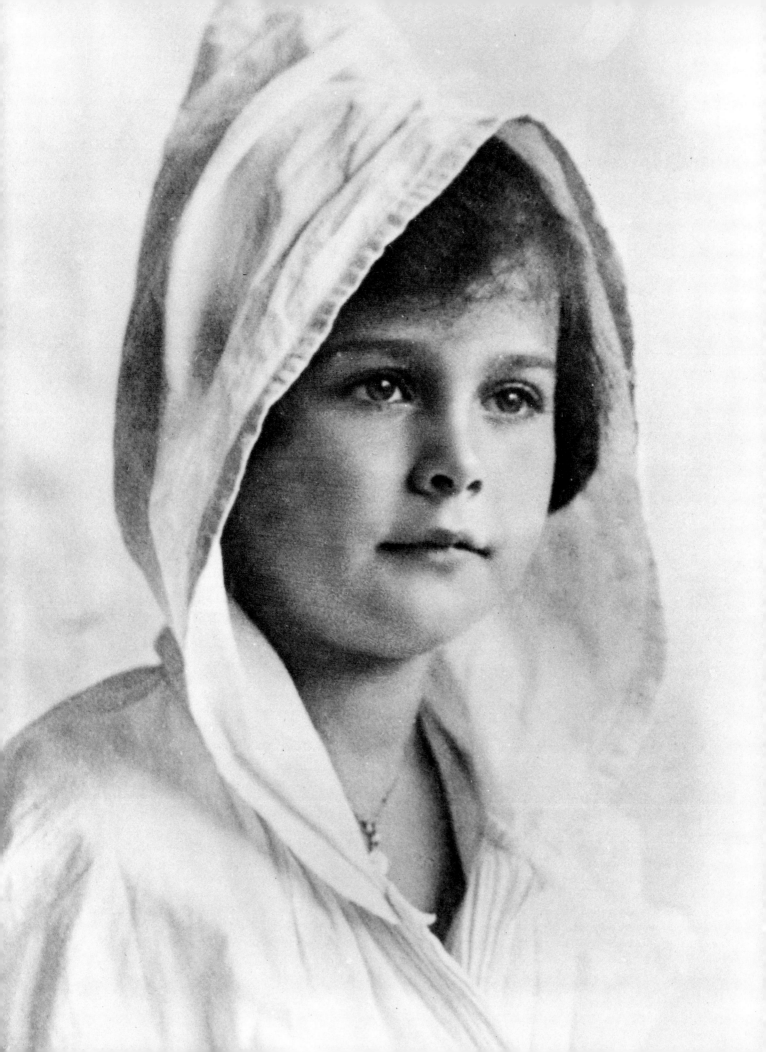

An only child, Hedy was the darling of her parents, who gave her everything that would make her happy. Her education was started when she was four. Private tutors taught her various subjects. She learned to speak several languages, including Hungarian, Italian, and English, and was given ballet and piano lessons.

The Kieslers lived in a luxurious house on the Peter Jordan Strasse in Vienna's fashionable 19th district. There they were often hosts to the most prominent and influential families in Europe, including businessmen, politicians, and royalty.

Whenever her parents went on business trips to London or Paris or Rome, they often took along Hedy and her faithful "Nanny," Nicolette. Later on, when barely in her teens, she was sent to a finishing school in Switzerland to learn the social graces.

During this time, she went on an Alpine hiking trip with classmates and met Ritter Franz von Hochestetten, son of a distinguished German family. A romance blossomed, and they became engaged. Hedy delayed the marriage, however, for she was becoming interested in a career in the theater. With her parent's permission, she enrolled in Max Reinhardt's dramatic school in Berlin. Reinhardt was so impressed with the young beauty that he immediately put her under his personal tutelage.

Young Ritter pleaded with her to marry him. When she refused and broke their engagement, the sensitive young man killed himself.

While studying in Berlin, she met Count Blucher von Wahlstatt, a descendant of the famous Prussian officer who had fought gallantly against Napoleon. Another engagement was announced, but her interest in the theater was stronger than her interest in Blucher, and the two went their separate ways.

Hedy began to get homesick, so she decided to leave Berlin and return to Vienna. There she continued her acting studies and took classes in art and design. (Later, she was to drive Hollywood designers mad by redesigning the clothes they had created for her.)

Hedy always had been a movie fan and read every screen magazine she could find. One morning in 1930, while walking to her classes, she decided to sneak into the Sascha film studio and watch what was going on.

Director Georg Jacoby, who was filming the company's first sound picture, *Geld auf der Strasse,* saw her. Impressed with Hedy's good looks and enthusiasm for films, he offered her a bit part, as a customer in a nightclub. To keep her on at the studio, Jacoby also gave her a job as script girl for the rest of the filming.

Jacoby's next film was *Sturm im Wasserglas,* based on a

Hedy at six

Hedy at seven

An Alpine vacation snapshot when she was 11 years old

The nine year old city "slicker"

play by Bruno Frank, which had been popular in Germany the year before. Hedy had made herself well known and well liked around the studio, so it was no surprise when she got a part in the new film. The role, that of a secretary in a newspaper office, was a minor one, but she made the most of it.

Through her studies and theatrical associates, she obtained a few stage roles at the Theater in der Josefstadt and at the Raimund-Theater. It wasn't long before she began getting larger roles in such plays as *The Weaker Sex* and *Private Lives.* The good reviews she was getting brought her to the attention of film director Karl Boese, who offered her the leading female role opposite Heinz Rühmann in *Wir Brauchen Kein Geld* (1931). The film received only fair notices, but Hedy's personal reviews were outstanding.

Everything seemed to be happening to her all at once. No sooner had she finished *Wir Brauchen Kein Geld* than Alexis Granowsky, the renowned Russian director, asked her to appear in *Die Koffer des Herrn O.F.,* a comedy he was about to film in Germany. He gave her the romantic lead opposite Harald Paulsen and signed Peter Lorre and Alfred Abel for the other starring roles. The amusing comedy premiered at the Mozart Saal in Berlin on January 17, 1932, before a very appreciative audience.

Then came *Ecstasy,* the film that caused a sensation all over Europe. Originally titled *Symphonie der Liebe,* it was called a masterpiece when it premiered in Prague. In the beginning, Hedy had doubts about doing the film. She would have to appear nude in two scenes and worried about the reaction of her parents. But she was ambitious and reasoned that if the picture was well received, her career would be assured.

Nudity is so common in movies today that it is hard to understand how so much fuss could be made over so little. Director Gustav Machaty seemed to have placed the camera a good half mile away for her famous nude swim and run through the woods.

But, in 1933, people were shocked at the thought of cameras witnessing anything so personal.

Perhaps even more shocking than the nudity were the facial expressions the camera recorded of her while in the throes of sexual pleasure with her lover.

Aribert Mog, playing a young engineer, was reported so madly in love with her that many wondered where acting stopped and reality began.

When the picture opened in Paris, the French audiences and critics alike exclaimed, "Ecstasy!" The producers were so pleased that they decided to retitle the picture.

Ecstasy was entered in the International Exhibition of

Already a radiant beauty at nine

Left: Looking sultry and wicked when she was a student in Berlin

Below left: Vamp . . Femme Fatale . . . La Prima Bella Donna . . . (Vienna, 1931)

Below: At the time of her engagement to Count Blucher von Wahlstatt

The young Madam Mandl in Salzburg, Austria, 1935

Attending the 1935 Vienna State Opera Ball. Hedy's first husband Friedrich (Fritz) Alexander Mandl is standing between Austrian Minister of Commerce Stockinger (smiling) and Major Baar von Bahrenfels (in uniform)

Cinematographic Art, which, in 1934, was still called the Cinematographic Biennial of Venice. By that time, Hedy had married, and her embarrassed husband objected so vigorously to showing *Ecstasy* that the angry judges awarded first prize for best foreign film to Robert Flaherty's *Man of Aran*.

The delegates did take an interest in *Ecstasy,* however, but not because of the scandalous publicity. The Cup of the City of Venice was awarded to director Gustav Machaty "for the great efficacy achieved with the simplest narrative art as well as to the understanding and spontaneous interpretation of nature."

Ecstasy was denounced by Pope Pius XI and banned in Germany by the Hitler regime. Several attempts to release the picture in the United States also failed.

Exhibitor Samuel Cummins finally received permission to show the film in New York after agreeing to cut out everything that a censorship committee found morally objectionable. So finally, in 1940, a bad print, scissored to appease a handful of prudes, opened to ice-cold reviews.

In recent years, since the end of censorship, *Ecstasy* has been restored in its entirety and shown to more sophisticated audiences, who are impressed with its symbolic art. Film historian Parker Tyler calls *Ecstasy* "unique" and "an impressionistic poem." Of Hedy, he says she was a "vision of lyric enchantment."

More famous than ever, Hedy returned to the Viennese stage in *Sissi,* a play based on the life of Elizabeth of Austria. It was while she was appearing in that play that Friedrich Alexander Mandl presented his card and came back stage for a visit. She was quite flattered, of course, for Herr Mandl was the owner of Hirtenberger Patronen-Fabrik Industries. Fritz, as he was called, was one of the four munition kings of the world. The others were Sir Basil Zaharoff, the international dealer in arms, Schneider-Creuzot, his French colleague, and Alfred Krupp, the master of the German cannon works in Essen.

Mandl had been married to Hella Strauss, a well-known Viennese actress. The marriage lasted two years. Shortly thereafter, a romance with German actress Eva May (the daughter of film star Mia May) caused a stir in social circles. Miss May killed herself over the affair, which she had described as hopeless. It seemed that Fritz had a yearning for young actresses!

Soon he was escorting Hedy around Vienna in his chauffeured limousine. There was a round of social functions that included the opera, the ballet, and dinner parties. When Mandl asked Herr Kiesler for the hand of his daughter, her father was delighted.

On the Vienna stage as Elizabeth of Austria in *SISSI* when she was nineteen

Hedy became Madam Mandl on August 10, 1933. The elaborate wedding took place in the Karlskirche, a magnificent baroque church and the most important building of its kind in Vienna. The church is only a short distance from the Belvedere Palace, in whose gardens Hedy had spent many girlhood hours wandering and daydreaming about the future. Those dreams seemed all to be coming true on that summer day in 1933.

Secure in her new life, she was not very concerned about politics; she left that to her husband. When Austrian Chancellor Dollfuss was murdered by the Nazis, she could not imagine the dark days that lay just ahead for Vienna and its people. She was too busy presiding over parties, which included some of the world's most famous people.

The Mandl guest list often included such names as Prince Gustav of Denmark, Prince Nicholas of Greece, Benito Mussolini, Madame Schiaparelli, Hungarian playwright Oedoen von Horvath, and writer Franz Werfel and his wife, who was the widow of composer Gustav Mahler.

Some early publicity relates that Hedy had entertained Adolf Hitler and that he had kissed her hand. As intriguing as it sounds, it never happened. She not only did not entertain the gentleman, she never even met him. Hardly, since she was married to Mandl, a Jew.

Hedy's life at that time can only be described as luxurious. She wanted for nothing—furs, jewels, limousines, a ten-room apartment in Vienna, and a mansion in Salzburg, where, it has been said, she ate from a solid-gold dinner service.

Mandl gave her everything. But he was a very jealous and possessive man who liked to wield power and who kept her a virtual prisoner.

The notoriety caused by *Ecstasy* infuriated him so much that he tried to buy up every existing print of the film and have it destroyed. After spending a small fortune, he discovered that the more prints he bought, the more turned up. His attempt to dispose of all existing prints was unsuccessful.

Hedy began to resent Mandl. While he was away on business trips, she would defy the servants, who were told to guard over her, slip out of the house, and rendezvous with an Austrian count, Ferdinand von Starhemberg. Using a key he had given her, she would slip into the royal palace. In November of 1936, Hedy and Count Ferdinand got on the Vienna-Budapest train together.

Mandl, who had been the chief armorer of Mussolini's expedition against Ethiopia, was in Rome selling munitions to the Spanish rebels. Notified by his spies of what was going on, he boarded a plane and flew to intercept the couple. He brought Hedy back to Vienna and had her guarded even more closely.

When the young count's brother, Prince Ernst Rudiger von Starhemberg, learned of Ferdinand's involvement with the married actress, the prince demanded that Ferdinand never see her again. The prince, moreover, was vice-chancellor of Austria. Between Mandl and the prince, Hedy knew what she was up against and realized that the affair was over. With the key now useless, she threw it into the Danube Canal.

By 1937, Hedy was becoming restless and tired of being locked away from the world. Hitler's power was growing, and she was finally becoming aware of what was happening in Europe.

Many German-Austrian film notables had already fled their homeland, or were about to flee, because they were Jews or because of the suppression of their artistic freedom. Among those who emigrated to America were actors Conrad Veidt, Peter Lorre, Marlene Dietrich, Paul Henried, Szöke (S. Z.) Sakall, Helene Thimig (Mrs. Max Reinhardt), Walter Slezak, Franz (Francis) Lederer, Felix Bressart, Albert Bassermann, Curt Bois, Mia May, and Marta Eggerth. Many of the finest directors also left: Fritz Lang, Henry Koster, Billy Wilder, Otto Preminger, Anatole Litvak, Wilhelm Dieterle, and Max Reinhardt.

Two of Hedy's early film associates were to become victims of the Nazis. Lovely Renate Müller (*Sturm im Wasserglas*) became intimately involved with Hitler in a sordid sexual affair. Because she unwisely bragged about it, she was hounded by the Gestapo and forced to commit suicide. She jumped from a hotel window in Berlin. Kurt Gerron (*Wir Brauchen Kein Geld*) was forced to make propaganda films for the government; and when his services were no longer needed, he was sent to Auschwitz and murdered.

Denied all opportunity to follow her career and with a marriage she could no longer endure, Hedy's one thought was to escape. "Whenever Mandl left Vienna," Hedy said, "I would be sent to our country estate to wait his return. I was constantly watched. I felt chained.

"I could bear it no longer, and carefully, day by day, I planned my escape. I knew to ask for my freedom would be fatal. So I watched and waited my chance. It came. My husband suggested we visit Antibes, and with my plan worked out, I agreed. My husband was called away on urgent business, and I said to the friends left to watch over me, 'Let's go to St. Wolfgang. It's much too warm here.' I was really longing for Salzburg and to see Max Reinhardt, but I knew better than to mention it, or I would arouse suspicion. So my friends agreed, and as Salzburg was only two hours' drive from St. Wolfgang, I was happy.

"One day I suggested, quite casually, we drive over to Salzburg. I didn't try then to contact Reinhardt but waited

A family gathering in Vienna. Seated: Hedy's maternal grandparents. Standing: Her uncle, mother Gertrud, father Emil, Hedy, and another uncle

my chance. Two days later, it came. A countess, who had a castle just out of Salzburg, asked me to visit her. My husband won't mind—she is a family friend, I insisted, and, at last, I was there as I had planned.

"The next night, we were invited to Reinhardt's to dinner. After the other guests had gone, we sat before the log fire and talked. I told him I had to get away, to get back to work."

"My dear," the great director said kindly, "you never will. It's all talk."

"But it wasn't," Hedy said. "I did get away. I went back to Vienna more determined than ever. Nothing could stop me."

She had no money of her own except a small amount saved from household expenses and a tiny sum she had managed to save to make ready for her flight. Her mother watched anxiously as she packed her luxurious clothes, fearing what Mandl would do if he caught her. All there was left to do was wait for the right opportunity.

And then, quietly, one night, while her husband was on a hunting trip in Hungary, with the aid of a faithful maid, she disguised herself as a servant, gathered up her luggage and all her jewels, and slipped out of the house. They sped to the Hauptbahnhof on the Mariahilfer Strasse, where she boarded the Trans-European-Express. She only began to feel a bit safer when the train crossed the Austrian border, the frontiers of Switzerland and France, until she finally arrived in Paris.

"It was torture to leave my mother behind," Hedy said. "I hurt my parents so deeply when I left our lovely home for the stage and screen. I saw my father's heart almost break over the mistake I was persuaded to make in *Ecstasy*. And yet I had to go."

It was during this hectic episode of her life that she received a wire from her mother telling of her father's death. She had never loved anyone as much as her father. It was, of course, impossible for her to return to Vienna, so she had to remain far from home and alone in her grief.

Believing that Paris was not quite far enough away to be completely safe from Mandl, she continued on to London. It was there where she met an American talent agent, Bob Ritchie, who took her to see his boss Louis B. Mayer, head of Metro-Goldwyn-Mayer. Mayer was on his famous European trip, which included attending the Paris premiere of *Camille* and looking for new faces for the movie company. He had already signed a lovely London stage actress, Greer Garson. Ilona Massey, a Hungarian blonde; Della Lind, another pretty blonde; and the opera star, Miliza Korjus, were also hired. The last three did not meet with favor with American audiences and soon faded from view.

Hedy had met Mayer once before when they were both guests at Max Reinhardt's baronial estate in Salzburg. Hedy, then married to Fritz Mandl, was trying to forget her romp through *Ecstasy*. Mr. Mayer, who had one standard for himself, set a different one for his stars. Although he found Hedy Kiesler Mandl to be exquisitely beautiful, he had seen *Ecstasy*, pronounced it as "dirty," and did not offer her any screen work. Hypocrite that he was, it was no secret around MGM that one of the great "lady" stars was his mistress for years.

The second meeting between the Viennese beauty and the MGM magnate was no more amiable than the first. In a crude remark, he informed her that Americans would not be interested in looking at her "ass." Hedy, practically in tears, was about to flee his hotel suite when Mayer changed his mind and offered her a six-month contract at $125 a week. Hedy regarded such a small amount as much an insult as his personal remarks, and turned it down.

Arriving in Los Angeles in 1937 to begin her American film career

In need of money, she was unwilling to part with any of her jewels. They might be a more needed asset later. She managed to get a job as governess to a child prodigy, Grisha Goluboff, who was about to sail for America.

Sailing aboard the *Normandie,* as a fellow passenger with her and the fourteen-year old violinist, was none other than Mr. Mayer! Before docking in New York, Hedy put on her most elegant gown and glittering diamonds and arranged another meeting with Mayer. A man not easily swayed, he was finally overcome by her loveliness. She not only wangled a decent contract out of the MGM chief for herself but one for young Grisha as well.

She arrived in the United States for the first time on September 30, 1937. After a few days of publicity in New York set up by MGM, she traveled by train to California to continue her film career.

Metro set Hedy and Ilona Massey up in a house in Hollywood. They were not only coached in acting and English but sent to all the film premieres and parties to make themselves better known in the film colony.

It was Mayer who changed Hedy's last name to Lamarr, in honor of the late silent-screen star Barbara LaMarr, whom he had admired. Everyone pronounced Hedy's name wrong (they said Heddy instead of Hay-dee), but she tried not to show how much it annoyed her.

At that time, Hedy, a staunch Catholic, appealed to the Holy Rota in Rome for an annulment of her marriage to Fritz Mandl. Her request was refused, and she went to Nevada and obtained a divorce.

Hedy ultimately made her American debut in *Algiers* (1938), a film that was a tremendous success and has become a minor classic.

But that occurred only after Metro had considered and discarded two scripts and a third production had shut down when Mayer quarreled with director Josef von Sternberg.

MGM had planned initially to debut Hedy in *Frou Frou,* Zoe Akins' revamp of an old Sarah Bernhardt success, already rejected by Luise Rainer. But this script was dropped, as was the studio's next project: a plan to star Hedy in *One Minute Alone,* from a screenplay by Dalton Trumbo. Gustav Machaty, the director of *Ecstasy,* would have been in charge.

Mayer, who wanted her American debut to be an important one, decided to guide it himself. He finally selected *I Take This Woman.* He chose Spencer Tracy as her leading man, cast Walter Pidgeon, Fanny Brice, Lana Turner, and Jack Carson in supporting roles, and signed Josef von Sternberg to direct.

A rare "cheesecake" photo taken while filming *ALGIERS*

With Mrs. Richard Tauber, Marlene Dietrich, Mrs. Gladys Peabody, Mrs. Charles Boyer (Pat Patterson) and Mrs. Douglas Fairbanks, Sr. (Sylvia Ashley) at a party given by Basil Rathbone at his Bel-Air estate, 1939

Celebrating the New Year 1939, with Charles Boyer

Visiting Joan Crawford on the set of THE WOMEN

Mayer had been so impressed by von Sternberg's molding of Marlene Dietrich's career that he felt the director could do the same for Hedy. But Mayer, constantly on the scene supervising "my Hedy Lamarr picture," caused von Sternberg so much trouble that the famed director, who was temperamental to begin with, quit in a rage.

Hedy's American debut came about because she met Charles Boyer at a party. Boyer was so entranced by her beauty that he urged producer Walter Wanger to negotiate with Metro to let Hedy appear with him in *Algiers.* Mayer, who never did anything for anyone without personal gain, agreed to loan Hedy for the film if Boyer would do one for him.

Wanger got the better bargain, for *Algiers* turned out to be very successful. (The picture Boyer made for Metro was *Conquest,* a dismal picture in which he played Napoleon, and one of Garbo's least successful pictures.)

With the release of *Algiers,* Hedy Lamarr became a star virtually overnight. *Ecstasy* had not yet been shown in the United States, and no one except the German community in New York had seen *Wir Brauchen Kein Geld.*

Critics went wild over her smoldering beauty, praised her performance as Gaby, and practically ignored Boyer. Magazines and newspapers fought for interviews with the brunette beauty.

Top stars even started emulating Hedy's high-bred ele-

Arriving at a Hollywood film opening with Louis Hayward and Ida Lupino, 1940

With second husband Gene Markey at the premiere of *JUAREZ* (Dolores Del Rio is in the background)

gance. Joan Crawford, who was having serious career problems, dyed her hair and parted it in the middle for her role in *The Ice Follies of 1939.* Blonde Joan Bennett also decided to switch to dark tresses, a flattering look familiar to viewers of her later movies.

Other dark-haired actresses also began to part their hair in the middle: Merle Oberon, Dorothy Lamour, Rosemary Lane, Eleanor Powell, and both Vivien Leigh and Olivia deHavilland in *Gone With The Wind.* Women everywhere were buying turbans and expensive costume jewelry, trying to look like the new star.

Although *Algiers* was definitely Hedy's picture, it received four Academy Award nominations for other people: Boyer, best actor; Gene Lockhart, best supporting actor; James Wong Howe, cinematography; and Alexander Tuluboff, interior decoration.

While Hedy was enjoying newfound success in America, Fritz Mandl was still in Austria and having problems with the Hitler government. Nazi authorities seized the properties and resources of the munitions king, and he fled to New York. Today, Mandl is an old man.* No longer bitter about the past, he lives on the Argentina Strasse in Vienna, not far from the Karlskirche, where he and Hedy were married.

When Mayer saw *Algiers,* he realized what an asset he had in Hedy and ordered the studio "build-up" for her. And there were to be no more loan-outs!

All of Hedy's publicity was costing Metro not a cent, so they planned to take advantage immediately by putting her to work in *Lady of the Tropics* with Robert Taylor. Taylor was no more than competent as an actor, but he was fresh from his leading role opposite Garbo in *Camille,* and female fans considered him the epitome of masculine good looks.

The people at Metro decided that putting the studio's two most attractive players together in one picture would be a pretty good idea. The picture was not memorable. Hedy movingly underplayed the tragic half-caste Manon, however, and gave a lovely performance.

Indeed, she is so good that one almost forgets that Taylor is even in the film. Joseph Schildkraut, although overshadowed by Hedy's presence, gave one of his best screen portrayals as the vengeful Delaroch, a supporting performance that has been overlooked and underrated.

Metro planned next to cast her in the star role in *Pocahontas,* opposite either Clark Gable or Spencer Tracy as Capt. John Smith. The idea seemed ludicrous to her; instead, she eloped with Gene Markey to Mexicali, where they were married in the governor's palace on March 5, 1939. Markey, a writer who had previously been married to Joan Bennett, moved from his bachelor quarters into

* Fritz Mandl died in 1977 at the age of seventy-seven.

Hedgerow, Hedy's newly acquired Beverly Hills mansion.

They started having marriage problems immediately and hoped that adopting a child might help. When they brought little James Lamarr Markey home, Hedy gave so much attention to the adorable boy that Markey felt neglected, and they were divorced within a year.

During the period after her divorce from Markey, Hedy was content just working and being a good mother to Jamie. She seldom socialized, but when she did, she was usually escorted by her good friend Reginald Gardiner, the one man she says she should have married but didn't.

Hedy's first legal tangle with MGM occurred late in 1939 when she announced that she would appear on the stage in *Salome.* Loew's Inc., with whom she was under exclusive contract, was granted a restraining order that prohibited her from going on with the play.

To make it even more difficult for her to appear on the stage, Metro reactivated production on *I Take This Woman.* Most of the original footage was scrapped, and except for Hedy and Spencer Tracy, a whole new cast was assembled. Walter Pidgeon, busy on another film, was replaced by Kent Taylor, Lana Turner by Laraine Day, Fanny Brice by Ina Claire, and Miss Claire in turn by Verree Teasdale.

One of MGM's busiest directors, W. S. Van Dyke, was called in to replace von Sternberg.

Although Hedy thought Tracy was a fine actor, she did not enjoy working with him. He mumbled a great deal, and she found him difficult to understand since she was not yet at ease speaking English. It would have been best if *I Take This Woman* had been forgotten in the first place, for it turned out to be one of the worst pictures ever made on the MGM lot. Tracy tried nobly under trying conditions, Hedy seemed completely zonked, and Verree Teasdale was allowed to ham outrageously.

By now Hedy needed a really good picture. She not only got one but two in a row. She knew that *Boom Town* was going to be an important picture and set out to get one of the top roles. Clark Gable and Spencer Tracy worked well together and were both outstanding, but Claudette Colbert was less exciting in a rather colorless part.

Hedy had the smaller but better female role and was excellent as the other woman. Her performance as the smart financial tipster was so good that had she been given supporting billing, she might have been an Oscar contender.

The picture did receive two nominations, for best cinematography and special effects. A Gallup poll also named *Boom Town* as the best-liked motion picture of 1940.

After *Boom Town,* Hedy and Clark Gable went right into *Comrade X.* This was her first chance to play comedy,

Appearing on the Lux Radio Theatre's production of *ALGIERS,* 1941

Going over costume sketches with designer Adrian on the set of *LADY OF THE TROPICS*

Lunching with Ann Sheridan and Ann Sothern during the filming of *H.M. PULHAM, ESQ.*

Visiting a Los Angeles children's hospital with Susan Hayward during a tour of Community Chest agencies by film stars, 1941

at which she proved herself most adept. The two had a great time working together in that fast-paced comedy about a Russian streetcar conductor (Hedy) and an American newspaperman (Gable) who whoop it up, much as Greta Garbo and Melvyn Douglas had the year before in the similar *Ninotchka.*

As the Russian girl with the improbable name of Theodore, Hedy discarded her usual glamorous outfits to wear a motorman's uniform. Except for a negligee and a bathrobe, she got to wear no other female attire.

Comrade X was a huge success, and Walter Reisch received an Oscar nomination for his delightful screenplay. Hedy enjoyed working with Gable, for whom she had great admiration; they harmonized well in both pictures they made together. The escape scene at the end of *Comrade X,* in which Hedy and Gable steal a tank to make their getaway, is one of the most hilarious chase scenes ever put on film.

Hedy was fast establishing herself as a superstar. Metro had her contract rewritten, guaranteeing her $25,000 per picture. The studio was quick to notice Hedy's talent for comedy in *Comrade X* and rushed her immediately into another.

In *Come Live with Me,* she played a refugee who wants to become an American citizen so badly that she is willing to pay someone to marry her. It is an enjoyable comedy, with Jimmy Stewart as the mildly amusing fellow who accepts her offer.

Hedy loved working with Stewart, and he became her favorite leading man. She remembers that he was very easygoing and very helpful to her. She was often bored with her leading men but never with Jimmy, whom she found to be extremely intelligent and very mechanically inclined.

Hedy and Stewart co-starred next in *Ziegfeld Girl* (1941), and both were sorry that they had no scenes together; he played opposite Lana Turner.

Ziegfeld Girl is a picture that Hedy practically begged to be in but ended up regretting because of the hard work in making it. At the time, she felt a musical would be a nice change of pace from what she had been doing. Neither a singer or dancer, she knew she had the good looks to be the most glorified girl of them all.

How right she was! When *Ziegfeld Girl* was being cast, she went to Louis B. Mayer and asked him to give her a part. Since Eleanor Powell had dropped out, and Mayer needed another marquee name, he decided to have one of the minor roles built up for Hedy.

Surrealist painting by Reginald Gardiner

Drawing by famed artist James Montgomery Flagg

29

Relaxing at her Beverly Hills home, Hedgerow

Her part was that of a girl who joins the Follies so she can help her down-and-out husband. Her role was not as important as those of Judy Garland and Lana Turner, but it was the most realistic and human of the three. She certainly was the most beautiful of the lot. She has never looked more stunning than she did then, gowned in the lovely creations of Adrian and photographed to perfection by cameraman Ray June.

Ziegfeld Girl was given a spectacular production and contained many dazzling musical presentations, the most glittering of which was the "You Stepped Out of a Dream" number. That and the "Trinidad" number were probably the best ever staged by the incomparable Busby Berkeley.

Ziegfeld Girl happens to be a favorite of this writer, but Hedy does not have fond memories of making it. She found working on the film to be most difficult. The costumes, which she had to wear for hours at a time, were heavy and tired her out, particularly the gown adorned with stars. A board had to be placed across her back to hold up the halo of stars around her head, and it exhausted her.

Her memories of Judy Garland are happy ones; they were, she recalls, "great pals." She does not remember, however, ever talking off camera with Lana Turner.

Ziegfeld Girl is a delight to watch today. Occasionally shown on television and periodically reissued in theaters, it seems so much better now than ever, probably because of the principal players and the nostalgia they evoke. Hedy was at her most beautiful; Judy was at her freshest; and it was this film that elevated Lana to stardom; she has never given a better performance.

Not only Hedy's fans but many critics as well believe that Hedy gave the best performance of her career as Marvin Myles, the sophisticated copywriter of John P. Marquand's *H. M. Pulham, Esq.* When Metro announced her for the plum role, no one who knew the story believed that Hedy could handle the role of the New York career girl.

Where was Katharine Hepburn? Surely, she would have been better. But Hedy proved the doubters wrong by turning in a splendid acting job.

Robert Young was also first-rate as Pulham and gave his best screen performance as well. Good support was given by Ruth Hussey as Pulham's wife, Charles Coburn as his father, and Van Heflin as the best friend. King Vidor's direction was impeccable.

The year 1942 was a very eventful one for Hedy. She had three films released, became engaged to marry, and was reunited with her mother after a separation of five years. Mrs. Kiesler had fled Austria. She made her way to England, then to California, where she has lived ever since.

With Lana Turner and Judy Garland on the set of
ZIEGFELD GIRL

With Jean-Pierre Aumont at a 1942 movie premiere

At the same time, Hedy announced that she would marry actor George Montgomery, later the husband of singer Dinah Shore. He was at 20th Century-Fox filming *Ten Gentlemen From West Point* with Maureen O'Hara, while Hedy was working with Spencer Tracy and John Garfield in *Tortilla Flat* at Metro. It was on the set of *Tortilla Flat* that their engagement picture was taken, with Hedy in her peasant costume. Montgomery was soon called into the service and found himself far from Hollywood. Hedy, meanwhile, kept herself busy in front of the cameras during the day and hurried home to spend the evenings with son Jamie.

War was raging in Europe and the Pacific. Hedy, like so many other Hollywood stars, lent her services to the war effort. She went on bond drives and helped build GI morale by entertaining at the Hollywood Canteen. She and her pal Ann Sothern danced with the boys, handed out donuts and coffee, or took their turns in the kitchen washing dishes.

It was at the Canteen on Christmas Eve, 1942, that Bette Davis, one of the stars who had helped organize the Canteen, introduced her to John Loder. He was an English actor who had just appeared with Miss Davis in *Now, Voyager*.

The two seemed to like each other and started dating, although many of their dates were no more than the sharing of duties at the Canteen. After a few months, they realized they were in love and decided to marry.

Hedy and Loder were married on May 27, 1943. The ceremony, performed in the Hollywood home of an old friend, Mrs. Conrad Veidt, was followed by a honeymoon at Lake Arrowhead. George Montgomery did not receive the usual "Dear John" letter. Instead, he learned from a newspaper story that his lovely fiancée had married someone else.

The first of Hedy's films to be released in 1942 was *Tortilla Flat*, based on John Steinbeck's best seller about *paisanos* on Monterey's Cannery Row. That delightful comedy provided Hedy with one of her favorite roles, that of the Portuguese girl Dolores, who packs fish in a sardine factory. The part gave her the chance to get out of high-fashion clothes and into peasant dresses, which she dearly loved.

Hedy still felt uncomfortable working with Spencer Tracy, but she did like working with John Garfield, whose acting she greatly admired. As good as the three stars were, it was Frank Morgan who stole the picture. Morgan, who usually overacted (as he had done with Hedy and Tracy in *Boom Town*), gave his greatest performance in *Tortilla Flat*. His poignant portrayal of the old hermit

whose only friends are his dogs earned him an Academy
Award nomination as best supporting actor.

Hedy's next film, *Crossroads*, was far from her best.
William Powell was cast as a diplomat suffering from am-
nesia, and Hedy played his loyal wife, who cannot believe
he is guilty of robbery and murder. The picture gave Hedy
little to do except stand around and wonder what would
happen next.

Powell, in a change of pace from his *Thin Man* roles,
seemed uncomfortable with his part, although he and
Hedy worked well together. *Crossroads* was often confusing and difficult to follow, as if much of it had been made
up as they went along. In the supporting cast, Basil Rathbone was particularly good as a blackmailer, and Felix
Bressart played his familiar role as the good doctor. But
Claire Trevor as a nightclub singer and Rathbone's cohort
had a ridiculous part.

The role of the central character in Leon Gordon's *White
Cargo*, the black sorceress Tondelayo, was coveted by
many Hollywood actresses. But Metro had Hedy in mind
from the beginning.

A number of well-known actresses have played Tondelayo since Earl Carroll first produced *White Cargo* in 1923.
Annette Margules and Betty Pierce each played the role
during its run of 104 weeks in New York, and several stock
companies later featured such names as Lili Damita, Ann
Corio, and Sally Rand.

But of all the Tondelayos, the one who is best remembered is Hedy Lamarr. Who will ever forget her entrance
through those bamboo curtains as she utters a sultry, "I
am Tondelayo."

Her performance could not have been better; every cat-
like move, every inviting gesture, was perfect. One could
almost read the cunning thoughts behind her alluring eyes.
Costumed by Kalloch in something called a "lurong" she
was a knockout as the native vixen. The musical score by
Bronislau Kaper was sultry and set the desired mood.

Walter Pidgeon was appropriately cynical as the overseer of a rubber plantation, Frank Morgan was better than
usual as a gin-soaked doctor, and Richard Carlson turned
in a polished performance as the weak husband who
couldn't hold Tondelayo.

Her role in *White Cargo* made Hedy a favorite of GIs in
army camps and foxholes everywhere. Photos of her in the
scanty sarong made her a popular pinup girl, competing
with such lovely gals as Ann Sheridan, Rita Hayworth,
Dorothy Lamour, and even adorable dimpled Betty
Grable.

Hedy's only film in 1943 was a mild little comedy in
which she was paired again with William Powell. She and

TWENTY COMPLETE STORIES FOR FIVE CENTS

Hollywood

(Reg. U. S. Pat. Off.)

MAY
NSC

A FAWCETT PUBLICATION
HOLLYWOOD
5¢

HEDY LAMARR
in a scene from
"ZIEGFELD GIRL"

BE AN AMERICAN

ARE SIN AND SEX HOLLYWOOD'S REAL TEMPTATIONS?
A Frank Answer By Cecil B. De Mille

One of the most popular cover girls of the 1940s

HOLLYWOOD

FEBRUARY

5¢

HEDY LAMARR

AR HOROSCOPES FOR 1942 BY NORVELL

PIC

WINCHELL VS. HITLER

COVERING THE ENTI

HEDY LAMARR

NOVEMBER 24, 1942 . PRICE TEN CENTS . TWELVE CENTS IN CANADA

The Smart Screen Magazine

SCREENLAND

October

15¢

HOW
HEDY
LAMARR
SOLVES
HER
LOVE
PROBLEMS

dy
arr

T MISS COMPLETE STORY OF DAMON RUNYON'S "THE BIG STREET"

PHOTOPLAY

combined with Movie Mirror

15¢

May

HEDY LAMAR
BY PAUL HESS

The Truth
about
THE STARS
IN SERVICE—
Facts on
Alan Ladd,
Tony Martin,
John Payne,
Glenn Ford

Powell had proved that they were a good team in *Cross-roads*, so Metro decided to star them together again in *Till You Return*, titled *The Heavenly Body* in final release. A pleasant little yarn about an astronomer who neglects his pretty wife, it did a good box-office business, mostly because of the drawing power of the two star names on the marquee.

Both carried off their assignments with routine work that did not require much from either of them. In the supporting category, Fay Bainter's talents were wasted, daft Spring Byington was out in left field, as usual, and James Craig was handsome.

While *The Heavenly Body* was in production, two other films were announced for Hedy: *Duel in the Sun* and *Dragon Seed*. But she lost the role in *Duel* when author Niven Busch abandoned plans for his own production and sold the property to David O. Selznick. Jennifer Jones took over Hedy's role as the half-breed Pearl Chavez and was nominated for an Academy Award.

About this time, Hedy was in the habit of turning down nearly everything, including *Gaslight*. And when Metro offered her the star role in Pearl Buck's best seller *Dragon Seed*, she refused it; she says she could not imagine herself as Jade, the Chinese heroine. Perhaps for spite, Metro refused to loan her to Warners for *Mr. Skeffington* or to Fox for *Laura*, two films for which she would have been ideally cast.

Turning down *Dragon Seed* was a mistake, for it was an important picture. Marguerite Roberts and Jane Murfin fashioned a good screenplay from the book, a huge cast of important actors was assigned prominent roles, and Sidney Wagner produced some superior photography. Katharine Hepburn inherited the part Hedy refused and gave one of her usual fine performances.

It has been said that Warner Brothers had tried to borrow Hedy from MGM for their production of *Casablanca*. Whether that is true or not, everyone knows that Ingrid Bergman got that choice part opposite Humphrey Bogart.

When Warners tried again for Hedy's services, they were more successful. Since Hedy was giving her home studio so much trouble by turning down so many films, they finally decided that getting her off the lot for a few weeks would be a good idea. *The Conspirators* was supposed to be another *Casablanca*. It wasn't.

The Conspirators was, nevertheless, an interesting picture of wartime intrigue. Hedy, cast as the wife of a double-agent, played by Victor Francen, was reunited with Peter Lorre, with whom she had worked in Germany eleven years previously in *Die Koffer des Herrn O. F.* Paul Henried, a friend from her Vienna days, was her leading man. Important supporting roles were well handled by Sydney Greenstreet, Joseph Calleia, and Eduardo Cianelli. Henried seemed to be repeating the exact role he had played in *Casablanca* and suffered just as intensely.

TEN CENTS EVERY WEEK *Movie and* RADIO GUIDE PROGRAM FOR JUNE 1-

HEDY LAMARR
First color photo of Hedy Lamarr as she will appear in M-G-M's "Boom Town"

Read the Story of "Brother Orchid" By Richard Connell
What Are the Chances of Having Television in Your Home in 1940

MOVIE STARS PARA
SEPTEMBER
15¢

HEDY LAMARR

$1,000 PRIZE CON

HEDY LAMARR
as she appears in
the M-G-M film
"Tortilla Flat"

But, as the mystery woman, Hedy was more interesting to watch. And the watching was quite easy; she looked absolutely ravishing in one gown after the other from the stunning wardrobe designed for her by Leah Rhodes.

Between 1940 and 1945, Hedy also worked in radio frequently. Some of the programs on which she appeared were the "Lux Radio Theatre," the "Screen Guild Players," "Star and Story," and the "Kay Kyser Show." She appeared on the Lux broadcasts of *The Bride Came C.O.D.* with Bob Hope and *Love Crazy* with William Powell and repeated her original roles in *Algiers* and *H. M. Pulham, Esq.*

Ironically, she got to do *Casablanca*, after all, starring with Alan Ladd and John Loder in its Lux presentation in 1944.

One picture Hedy regretted turning down was *Gaslight*, for which Ingrid Bergman won her first Oscar. After she saw how good it was, Hedy jumped at RKO's offer to star in *Experiment Perilous*. It was a psychological mystery of the sort that studio was known for. Although not as good as *Gaslight*, *Experiment Perilous* did turn out to be a fine film; Hedy gave a glowing performance as the adored Allida.

George Brent was as bland as usual, but Paul Lukas, who had just won an Academy Award for his performance in *Watch on the Rhine*, added not only prestige to the picture but a fine acting job as well. The doomed sister-in-law, Cissy, was admirably played by Olive Blakeney, a talented actress whom Hedy thought should have become more famous.

Experiment Perilous, based on a novel by Margaret Carpenter, was Hedy's second loan-out in a row from Metro. Besides providing her with one of her best roles to date, it gave her a chance to wear beautiful turn-of-the-century costumes. She was also given a completely new hair style, lightened to a very becoming shade of red. As one of the most beautiful women of her time, she played a very sympathetic part and delivered what many consider her best performance. Her fans hoped she might get an Academy Award for the part. But she did not, for World War II was a period for actresses. With the best actors at war, the best parts were written for women, and there were just too many in competition.

Hedy's next film, *Her Highness and the Bellboy,* was done back on the Metro-Goldwyn-Mayer lot. It is a picture that she dislikes so much that she prefers not even to discuss it. It was a project that had been planned as far back as 1942, with Hedy as the princess and Mickey Rooney as the bellboy.

By the time it finally reached the screen, Rooney had been replaced by Robert Walker. Mickey Rooney must be thankful to this day!

It was a silly story about a bellboy who thought a princess was in love with him. With the exception of June

The official engagement photo of Hedy and George Montgomery taken on the set of *TORTILLA FLAT*, 1942

Attending a 1942 military ball at the Hollywood Palladium with Marion Davies, George Montgomery, William Randolph Hearst, Rita Hayworth and Lou Costello (behind Hearst)

Allyson in a sympathetic role, the rest of the cast did not fare well.

Walker was silly as the bumbling bellhop, and "Rags" Ragland's dumbbell was so ridiculous as to be totally unbelievable.

Hedy, pregnant with her first child, was so uncomfortable with the whole thing that she was indifferent to the fate of the picture. She was embarrassed with the result and so unhappy with the roles she was being offered by Metro that she asked to be released from her contract.

Hedy gave birth to her first child on May 29, 1945, at Cedars of Lebanon Hospital in Los Angeles. She named her daughter Denise Hedwig Loder in a christening ceremony attended by her husband and the child's godmother, Bette Davis. Loder then adopted Hedy's son James and changed the boy's last name from Markey to Loder.

Hedy was away from the cameras for over a year after the birth of her baby. She had committed herself to star in *Last Year's Snow* for producer Arnold Pressburger on a free-lance basis. She had known Pressburger when they were both working at Sascha in Vienna and was eager to start the assignment.

She was forced to cancel the deal, however, when she learned that she was pregnant. She was still in the middle of *Her Highness and the Bellboy* at the time and knew that before another picture was completed, her figure would show too much. Pressburger sued her for breach of contract, but the matter was settled out of court.

Since she was free from MGM, Hedy decided that she would produce her own pictures. Her partners in the venture were producers Hunt Stromberg and Jack Chertok. The company purchased two stories, *There's Always Love* and *The Immortal Smile,* in which Hedy would star.

Both stories, however, were discarded in favor of *The Strange Woman,* a best seller by Ben Ames Williams. It turned out to be a wise decision, providing Hedy with one of her best roles to date.

The story, set in Bangor, Maine, in 1820, gave her the chance to play the wicked Jenny Hager, one of the most evil bitches in modern literature. The film was given a sumptuous production, with magnificent sets erected to resemble the Maine logging town, and exquisite period costumes.

Hedy's performance was one of the best of her career, with only one jarring note. One was always aware of the Viennese accent instead of the necessary Down East drawl.

Gene Lockhart was excellent as her aged husband, as was Hillary Brooke as her best friend. But George Sanders, of all people, was miscast as a Maine lumberjack. The direction was handled with a certain flair by Edgar Ulmer, who had worked with Max Reinhardt in Europe. One can only wonder why such a lavish production was not filmed in color, a common process by that time.

The Strange Woman made bundles at the box office.

With John Loder at the 1943 premiere of *IN WHICH WE SERVE*

Rehearsing a radio show with Bing Crosby, James Cagney and Kay Kyser

With Alan Ladd and John Loder on the Lux Radio Theatre's broadcast of *CASABLANCA*, 1944

During World War II Hedy was a tireless worker at the Hollywood Canteen, where she helped to boost the morale of the lonely G.I.s

Because of the success of her first independent venture, Hedy was eager to start work on another picture immediately. She chose next to do *Dishonored Lady,* a story about a beautiful but despondent magazine editor, based on a true murder case. Katharine Cornell and Joan Crawford had appeared in earlier stage and screen versions. Hedy's version is the least memorable of the three. Due to the strict production code of the time, the story was heavily censored and the nymphomania of the central character written out of the script.

Hedy's performance was one-dimensional, although she did see to it that she got to wear pretty clothes as usual. She had talked her husband, John Loder, into playing the role of a wealthy jeweler who gets murdered, and hired Dennis O'Keefe for the other lead, but got little support from either. Natalie Schafer and Margaret Hamilton, in lesser roles, contributed their usual touch of "camp," and William Lundigan was only adequate as the weakling turned murderer.

Dishonored Lady was badly received and barely made back the money that it cost to make it. The headaches involved in running her own company were more than Hedy had anticipated or could cope with, so she decided to dissolve the association. It was just as well, for during the filming of *Dishonored Lady,* she discovered that she was pregnant again. Her son Anthony John Loder was born March 1, 1947.

Her marriage to Loder had been deteriorating long before this, and in July, she started divorce proceedings. Part of the blame for the failure of the marriage perhaps was because Loder was seventeen years older than Hedy. Loder's son by a previous marriage, Robin, was almost as old as his lovely stepmother. She complained that her husband fell asleep all the time and never talked to her. Hedy had desperately wanted the marriage to work and today speaks of Loder with fondness, describing their union as having been a "good match."

After the birth of her son, Hedy was off the screen for a year. Her divorce had also become final, and during this time, there was a brief romantic interlude with Mark Stevens. He was a popular actor at the time who made several films at 20th Century-Fox, among them a couple of pretty Technicolor musicals with June Haver.

The affair did not last long, nor did Stevens' career. He soon left Hollywood and went to Majorca, where he became a tennis instructor. Hedy was next involved romantically with wealthy businessman Herbert Klotz. That lasted long enough only for the announcement of their engagement. Hedy Klotz?

After two heavy dramas and the demise of her produc-

(OVERLEAF)
The M-G-M Family of Stars with their boss Louis B. Mayer. Left to right, *first row:* James Stewart, Margaret Sullavan, Lucille Ball, Hedy Lamarr, Katharine Hepburn, Mayer, Greer Garson, Irene Dunne, Susan Peters, Ginny Simms, Lionel Barrymore.

Second row: Harry James, Brian Donlevy, Red Skelton, Mickey Rooney, William Powell, Wallace Beery, Spencer Tracy, Walter Pidgeon, Robert Taylor, Jean-Pierre Aumont, Lewis Stone, Gene Kelly, Jackie "Butch" Jenkins.

Third row: Tommy Dorsey, George Murphy, Jean Rogers, James Craig, Donna Reed, Van Johnson, Fay Bainter, Marsha Hunt, Ruth Hussey, Marjorie Main, Robert Benchley.

Fourth row: Dame May Whitty, Reginald Owen, Keenan Wynn, Diana Lewis, Marilyn Maxwell, Esther Williams, Ann Richards, Martha Linden, Lee Bowman, Richard Carlson, Mary Astor.

Fifth row: Blanche Ring, Sara Haden, Fay Holden, Bert Lahr, Frances Gifford, June Allyson, Richard Whorf, Frances Rafferty, Spring Byington, Connie Gilchrist, Gladys Cooper.

Sixth row: Ben Blue, Chill Wills, Keye Luke, Barry Nelson, Desi Arnaz, Henry O'Neill, Bob Crosby, "Rags" Ragland.

Absent M-G-M stars were Judy Garland, Joan Crawford, Clark Gable, Margaret O'Brien, Kathryn Grayson, Lana Turner, Van Heflin, Ann Sothern, Myrna Loy, Laraine Day, Lew Ayres, Robert Young, Lena Horne, Virginia O'Brien.

tion company, Hedy decided that what she needed was a comedy. She then accepted the role of a lady psychiatrist, opposite Robert Cummings in *Let's Live a Little,* a little farce made by Eagle-Lion that did nothing for either of their careers. Hedy, however, had to wait only a year for her greatest success, *Samson and Delilah.*

She also canceled plans made at this time to appear in producer Albert Zugsmith's *Hideaway House.* (Zugsmith later was to become well known for his sexploitation films with Mamie Van Doren.)

Instead, she planned to move to New York and appear on the Broadway stage in *A Legend of Good Women,* a comedy by Maurice Vallency.

But this arrangement also fell through, and she landed her most important role just as her career was going into a swift decline. When Cecil B. DeMille started work on *Samson and Delilah* early in 1949, he could think of no one better suited than Hedy to play the seductive dame who gave Samson his famous clipping. She had worked with the legendary director on several Lux Radio Theatre broadcasts and was eager to do the film, which she knew would be monumental.

She was perfect as Delilah and perfectly beautiful in Edith Head's fabulous costumes. DeMille personally gathered peacock feathers from the birds on his farm to make up one of her lavish gowns.

Hedy considers her performance as Delilah the best of her career and *Samson and Delilah* the best film in which she ever appeared. Critics generally agree. Her performance was definitely the main asset of the film, one for which she deserved an Academy Award nomination. She was not only beautiful but cunning, tempting, vicious and greedy when necessary, and remorseful as well.

Victor Mature was quite acceptable as the massive Samson. George Sanders, who seemed to be in his glory, was appropriately nasty as the Saran of Gaza. Blonde Angela Lansbury, on the other hand, was miscast as Delilah's sister, and the dialogue given to the minor players was at times so painful as to make one cringe. Regardless of some minor flaws, *Samson and Delilah* was a colossal success. Hedy's first color film, it became one of the all-time money making films.

Hedy denies rumors that she and DeMille did not get along. In fact, they got along so well that when DeMille was casting *The Greatest Show on Earth,* he offered her the leading role of the trapeze artist that finally went to Betty Hutton. It was a part that required very strenuous work, which she turned down in favor of spending more time with her children.

DeMille still wanted to do another film with her and

The Loders with Bette Davis at the christening of their daughter, Denise Hedwig

Holding her son Tony on his first birthday

Hedy's name was used to promote a variety of products, which included perfume, make-up, soda drinks and cigarettes

46

Natural Color Photograph by Paul Hesse—Hollywood

To Maybelline—
The eye make-up I find
So truly flattering—
Always
Hedy Lamarr

Exchanging marriage vows with band leader Ernest (Ted) Stauffer before Judge Stanley Mosk in Los Angeles, 1951

proposed a grand production of *Thais,* but Hedy could not be persuaded.

Louis B. Mayer was so impressed with her performance as Delilah that he was willing to meet her financial terms when she decided to work again. Hedy did not like Mayer and resented his years of ill treatment.

Now in a bargaining position, she made the old man squirm by asking for a fee of $90,000. Knowing that the Lamarr name was good box office, he not only agreed to her asking price but also to a four-week shooting schedule.

She returned to the Metro lot after a five-year absence to make *A Lady Without Passport.* It was a property that she did not care for. She had already turned down *Father of the Bride* because she did not want to work with Spencer Tracy again and thought herself too young to play Elizabeth Taylor's mother. Since her other demands had been met, she decided not to have any more hassles. As a stranded refugee lingering in Havana, she was given little to do but look attractive in a few pretty dresses, while John Hodiak was given more footage and George Macready the best dialogue.

Paramount had been so pleased with the results of *Samson and Delilah* that they contracted Hedy for two more pictures. The first was *Copper Canyon,* a Western filmed in color with an Arizona setting. Her Viennese accent seemed wrong for the saloonkeeper from New Orleans, and she looked out of place in curls and ante-bellum costumes.

Likewise, Ray Milland, who was more at home in an English drawing room, was not a good choice for the fast-drawing Western hero. Nevertheless, Hedy liked making the film and working with Milland. She seldom got the opportunity to go on location for a picture and enjoyed the time the company spent in Arizona.

Copper Canyon was well mounted, and the beautiful Technicolor photography by Charles B. Lang, Jr., was an asset. Since Westerns were as popular as ever, it did a good business at the box office.

In her next film, *My Favorite Spy,* she fared much better; her talent for comedy was put on display again opposite Bob Hope. It was a very funny picture, which Hedy feels would have been even better had some of her best scenes not ended up on the cutting room floor.

When Hope asked her to become his leading lady in the picture, she jumped at the opportunity. Much to Hope's chagrin, she came off better than he in many of their scenes. Because of that, she believes he had many of her best scenes cut from the final print. This has always angered her, and to this day, she never has a pleasant word for the ski-nosed comedian.

Hedy Lamarr paper dolls were a popular children's item, as were coloring books and pencil tablets with her picture on the cover

Hedy began to tire of picture making and made one of her many retirement announcements. She took her children to Acapulco for a vacation and met former band leader Ernest (Ted) Stauffer there. He owned La Perla, a smart nightclub hangout for tourists in that Mexican resort, and had been married to another actress, Faith Domergue. Hedy married Stauffer in Los Angeles on June 12, 1951. He hoped that she would enjoy living in Acapulco. But she hated the heat, found the food unbearable, and "got awfully tired just sitting down there doing nothing." They were divorced a year later.

Unfortunately, Hedy did not make the next film that she had planned to do; 20th Century-Fox had offered her Ernest Hemingway's *The Snows of Kilimanjaro* with her friend Susan Hayward and Gregory Peck.

Since Hedy and Hayward had no scenes together, Hayward's scenes were filmed first. Then Hedy decided against the part, and it went to Ava Gardner, who gave one of the best performances of her career. Rumor has it that Hayward was furious when Ava got the part and would have refused to appear in the film if she had known Hedy would turn the part down.

Hedy, who had lived in the United States for many years, became a citizen on April 10, 1953, in Los Angeles.

As if she had not learned her lesson in producing her own films, she tried the same course again in 1953. She gained the backing of Texas oil man W. Howard Lee and went to Italy to make a picture that never was released in America. The film was called *Eterna Femmina* during a limited European release and ended up on U.S. television years later as a trilogy called *The Love of Three Queens.*

The venture was disastrous. She and the other investors lost a great deal of money on the project. To make matters worse, she was sued by lawyers who had represented her during legal problems concerning the ill-fated picture.

Hedy and Lee were married in New York at the Queens County Courthouse on December 22, 1953. He took her to Houston to live, a place she came to detest.

"How anyone who has seen anything of the world can live in Texas is beyond me," she said.

She was not accepted by his family. To get away, she suggested he buy a place in Aspen, Colorado. Since they were both avid skiers, he consented. The lodge he built cost $300,000 and was called the Villa Lamarr.

Hedy remained away from the camera for four years, trying to content herself with just being Mrs. Lee. When producer Irwin Allen offered her a cameo role in *The Story of Mankind* (1957), she decided to accept since it would not take long to film her segment. It was a curious picture, with bizarre casting, and did very badly in the few bookings it got.

Receiving her American Citizenship papers in Los Angeles, April 10, 1953

With Howard Lee on their wedding day, 1953

Hedy was seen as Joan of Arc in the longest episode in the picture. She had more footage than some of the other stars, who were on and off the screen so fast one had trouble spotting them. She received top billing, along with her old friend Ronald Colman.

Many others in the film were also old friends or former co-stars. Her dear friend Reginald Gardiner played Shakespeare; Edward Everett Horton, from *Ziegfeld Girl,* was a wild choice for Sir Walter Raleigh; Agnes Moorehead, the countess in *Her Highness and the Bellboy,* was a believable Queen Elizabeth I; Peter Lorre, with Hedy in both *Die Koffer des Herrn O.F.* and *The Conspirators,* gave some conviction to his role of Nero; fellow Viennese actor Helmut Dantine was Mark Antony; and the tragic Cathy O'Donnell, who had been in *Eterna Femmina,* had a bit part.

In her last film, *The Female Animal,* Hedy looked too young to play Jane Powell's mother. In reality, she is only fifteen years older than Miss Powell. Overcoming an inept script, Hedy, in the role of a famous movie star with an eye for younger men, managed to outplay the other members of the cast.

Miss Powell looked tired and overacted. George Nader, a last-minute replacement for John Gavin, looked terrific but seemed embarrassed with his sexy he-man role. Jan Sterling played competently in a bitchy part as a rival actress who also likes her men on the younger side of thirty.

In the same year that she made her last film, 1957, Hedy made her dramatic television debut. She was a guest star on the "Zane Grey Theatre" in an episode called *Proud Woman.* In it, she played the role of a woman who takes over the management of a ranch when her father becomes incapacitated.

Hedy's marriage to Howard Lee, which she has described as "the darkest chapter in my life," became so intolerable that she separated from him in August 1958. She was granted a divorce in April 1960 and awarded a settlement of $500,000, of which she swears she never received a cent. She became so distraught during the divorce action that she came down with pneumonia and had to send her stand-in, Sylvia Hollis, to court to testify for her.

In 1963, she was to have appeared in a CBS television special called "The Man Who Bought Paradise." An all-star cast also was to include Robert Horton, Angie Dickinson, and Buster Keaton.

One could almost have predicted the outcome: Last-minute details between Miss Lamarr and the network could not be worked out. Whether the dispute was over billing or salary, it was not made known. Salary, however,

With Lewis Boies, husband number six, at a preview of
THE CHALK GARDEN

would be the better guess. At any rate, Hedy was replaced by another great beauty, Dolores Del Rio.

Hedy's lawyer during her court battles with Lee was Lewis J. Boies. He became so infatuated with his client that he began sending her flowers and gifts and finally asked her to marry him. She consented, and they were married in Fresno, California, on March 4, 1963. The marriage lasted two years.

She was granted her sixth divorce on June 21, 1965, after her teen-age son testified that it had been a "destructive relationship."

Tony said that he had seen Boies push his mother on occasion and threaten her with a baseball bat. Hedy said that she had spent "about a half million dollars" on her husband, money raised by selling paintings from her valuable art collection.

The saddest chapter in her life occurred when she was arrested on a shoplifting charge on January 28, 1966. She was accused of taking $86 worth of cosmetics and clothing from The May Company department store in Los Angeles. She said she had only stepped out of the store to summon her business manager to pay for the items.

Because she was a star, she was accustomed to paying for all purchases at once instead of individually. Hedy suffered the indignity of being jailed for five hours before bail money arrived. At the time of the arrest, she was carrying $13 in cash and two checks totaling $14,000.

She was accompanied to the Sybil Brand Institute, a detention center for women, by her business manager, Earl Mills. Asked about the charges lodged against her, she said that it was all a misunderstanding. But she was booked under the name Hedy Boies and told to appear in Division 59 of Los Angeles Municipal Court on February 2 at 1 P.M.

Her son Tony told reporters, "For the past thirty years my mother has been doing a great deal for the United States and the people in it, and in return she has received a slap in the face—for nothing. I mean, she has given a lot to everyone even when she was above everyone in fame and recognition.

"During the past ten years, she has been more or less down and out; she's had her own problems off the screen. The divorces do upset her a great deal, more than anyone can imagine. And since she is in this condition, no one looks after her or takes care of her, as she has done for others."

Denise also defended her mother by saying, "These last ten years have been a constant strain on my mother both financially and emotionally. You know, in just one day during World War II, my mother sold more than seven million dollars worth of bonds."

With daughter Denise and son-in-law Lawrence Colton at the couple's wedding in Beverly Hills, 1965

With noted film critic Rex Reed on *THE MIKE DOUGLAS SHOW* in 1969

With her son Tony during the trial in Los Angeles, 1966

Hedy Lamarr in the 1970s

In a much-publicized trial, Hedy took the stand to tell of her health and career problems and the loss of her money and property. The jury, who seemed in awe of the famous star, pronounced an emphatic verdict of "not guilty." Thus, amid the applause of the spectators in the courtroom, ended weeks of mental pain inflicted upon her.

Because of the shoplifting fracas, Hedy was too fatigued to start work on her first picture in years and was fired. She had signed to co-star with Don Ameche in *Picture Mommy Dead*. Producer Bert I. Gordon claimed that because of high production costs he could not await Miss Lamarr's availability. He replaced her with Zsa Zsa Gabor. Gene Tierney, who is married to Hedy's ex-husband Howard Lee, had also been a contender for the part.

Hedy has since refused starring roles in two films to concentrate on her $2-million lawsuit against The May Company store for false arrest. Columnist Sheila Graham once suggested that she drop the suit.

"Oh, no—I was acquitted, but I have not acquitted them," she replied. "It was an emotional thing for me. I still can't go into a store without shaking.

"The way they treated me!

"You know, I had a check for fourteen thousand dollars in my pocket. No, I shall enjoy this appearance in court."

After all these years, she is still involved in litigation, and no settlement has been made.

At present, Hedy isn't interested in acting and turns down the offers that she continues to receive. Not too long ago, she was asked to appear in a stage production of *The Killing of Sister George,* a London and New York stage success that was made into an interesting film.

But one screen role in recent years would have interested her, she says, that of the countess in *Something for Everyone.*

She would have been just right as the Austrian countess in *The Sound Of Music*. One can only wonder why she wasn't approached to play the part. But it was done by Eleanor Parker, a fine actress who was too American for the role.

Recently, an interviewer asked her how it felt to be a beautiful woman.

"I was really never aware of being beautiful. I never thought about it, and I never had any ego problems," she said. "I'm just like anyone else with two eyes and a nose and mouth. I do, however, have my own nose and my own teeth.

"I believe in simplicity and inner beauty—I can find something beautiful about all the people I like. What's important is to be yourself and be accepted as such—not what you look like. A person just can't live by relying on outer beauty—it fades.

"Once in a while I have a glimpse of myself, and I think I'm quite good-looking. My mother always said to be beautiful all the time, and that instantly made me subconsciously not want to be. Some rely on beauty, but I don't. If you do, you're dead."

Hedy has always been close to her family and sees them as often as possible. Her son Tony, a photographer, lives in West Los Angeles. Her mother "Trude" lived with him there until her death in 1977. Tony, twice married, has two children, the older of whom, Lodi, lives with her mother in Paris. Hedy's daughter Denise, also a beautiful woman, is a model in Seattle, where she resides with her own daughter Wendy. Hedy's older son James, a policeman in Nebraska, made headlines himself a few years ago after accidentally shooting a black girl during the outbreak of a race riot in Omaha.

Today, Hedy Lamarr lives in an apartment on New York's fashionable East Side and spends much of her time now going to the movies, listening to lectures, roaming the art galleries, and painting. She is a good artist herself and has had her work exhibited in many of the better galleries in New York, Los Angeles, and Houston.

She enjoys winter vacations in Aruba and other Caribbean resorts, where she is often joined by Denise. Many summer weekends are spent with friends at Sag Harbor or Fire Island, delighting them with amusing stories and anecdotes. She is completely happy living in the East and seems glad to be away from the Hollywood scene.

Still sleek and lovely, Hedy has conquered several bouts with pneumonia and two serious eye operations. From time to time, the daily trade papers continue to report that Hedy will emerge from retirement to accept another film role, but as pleasant as it would be to see her on the screen again, it is quite unlikely. Perhaps she no longer has the desire to ever make another film. If so, that is understandable.

Time, to be sure, has tempered the image that once evoked cries of "Ecstasy!" It cannot, however, temper the vision of beauty and excitement preserved for us in the films of Hedy Lamarr.

In her New York apartment with Christopher Young

THE TRANSCENDENT BEAUTY

She walks in beauty, like the night
Of cloudless climes and starry skies,
And all that's best of dark and bright
Meet in her aspect and her eyes

Lord Byron

THE FILMS OF
HEDY LAMARR

GELD AUF DER STRASSE
MONEY ON THE STREET
A Sascha-Film Production   (Austrian—1930)

With Georg Alexander (seated), Alfred Neugebauer (policeman), Lydia Pollmann and Hans Thimig (wearing glasses)

CREDITS

Directed by Georg Jacoby. *Produced by* Nikolaus Deutsch. *Screenplay by* Rudolf Oesterreicher. *Based on a play by* Rudolf Bernauer *and* Rudolf Oesterreicher. *Director of Photography,* Nikolaus Farkas. *Art Direction by* Hans Jacoby. *Music by* Stephan Weiss. *Music arranged by* Frank Fox. *Song, "Lach mich nicht, weil ich Dir so treu bin!" by* Peter Herz *and* Stephan Weiss. *Photograph direction by* Robert Leistenschneider *and* W. Sturmfeld. *Sound editor,* Alfred Norkus.

CAST

Peter Paul Lutz, GEORG ALEXANDER; *Emil Reimbacher,* LEOPOLD KRAMER; *Lona Reimbacher,* ROSA ALBACH-RETTY; *Dodo,* LYDIA POLLMANN; *Albin Jensch,* HANS MOSER; *Mr. Kesselberg,* HUGO THIMIG; *Max Kesselberg,* HANS THIMIG; *Bornhausen,* FRANZ SCHAFHEITLIN; *Dallibor,* KARL ZIEGLER; *Lukas,* ERNST ARNOLD; *Tschakowa,* ROSE MATHÉ; *Policeman,* ALFRED NEUGEBAUER; *Bookkeeper,* WILHELM HEIM; *Head Waiter,* HERMANN WAWRA; *Manager,* FRANZ KAMMAUF; *Singer in the Carlton Bar,* HARRY PAYER; *Young Girl,* HEDY KIESLER

SYNOPSIS

Dodo, the daughter of a banker, is to marry Max Kesselberg, a narrow-minded young man. Everyone is assembled for the engagement announcement; only one person is missing, the bride-to-be herself.

She is with the famous tenor, Dallibor, whom she has seen on the stage and idolizes. She begs the singer to run away with her.

But Dallibor has other things on his mind than satisfying the whims of a young girl. Disappointed, she leaves the man she had adored.

On the street, she meets the well-traveled Peter Paul Lutz. He considers himself a lucky man and maintains the theory that money may be found lying on the street. One needs only to pick it up.

Peter, with his philosophy of life, proves to be not so wrong after all; with Dodo, whom he so unexpectedly has met, he acquires not only love and happiness but also riches.

Through her, he gains possession of an important telegram, from which he learns that the stock of a big mine in America is going up. Dodo's uncle owns a portfolio of the stock he considers worthless, and Peter obtains it for a trifle. Dodo breaks her engagement to Max and marries Peter, who has become a rich man.

NOTES

Hedy was only an observer on the set of *Geld auf der Strasse* when she was spotted by director Georg Jacoby, who thought she was pretty enough to dress up a night-club scene that he was about to shoot. Sitting at a table, wearing a black evening gown, with the camera turning, gave Hedy her first taste of movie making. That was it. From then on, she wanted no other career.

Geld auf der Strasse, photographed by one of Europe's finest cameramen, Nikolaus Farkas, was the first sound film to be made by the Sascha studio. The cast was a prominent one, headed by such well-known German stars as Georg Alexander, Leopold Kramer, and Hans Moser. Kramer later played Hedy's father in *Ecstasy.*

Hedy (sitting in front of camera on the set) doubling as script girl

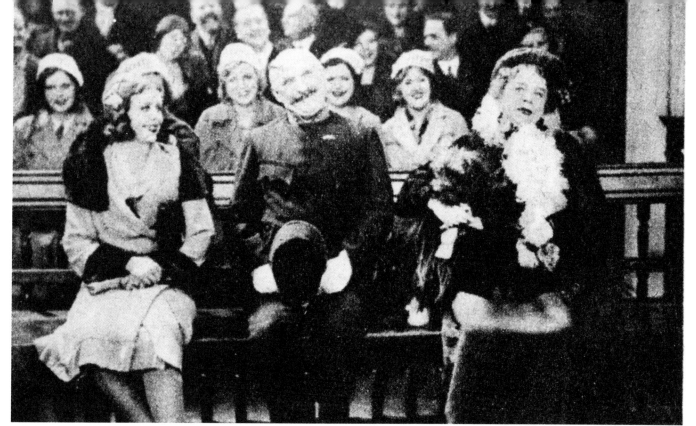

With Renate Muller, Oscar Szabo and Hansi Niese. Hedy is in second row, left

STURM IM WASSERGLAS
STORM IN A WATER GLASS

Also known as

DIE BLUMENFRAU VON LINDENAU
THE FLOWER WOMAN OF LINDENAU

A Sascha-Felsom Film Production   (Austrian
—1931)

CREDITS

Directed by Georg Jacoby. *Based on a play by* Bruno Frank. *Screenplay by* Walter Wassermann, W. Schlee *and* Felix Salten. *Photography by* Guido Seeber *and* Bruno Timm. *Running time, 70 minutes.*

CAST

Frau Vogel, HANSI NIESE; *Victoria,* RENATE MÜLLER; *Dr. Thoss,* PAUL OTTO; *Burdach,* HARALD PAULSEN; *Quilling,* HERBERT HUEBNER; *Lisa,* GRETE MAREN; *Dog Catcher,* OSCAR SZABO; *Judge,* OTTO TRESSLER; *Prosecutor,* FRANZ SCHAFHEIT-LIN; *Burdach's secretary,* HEDY KIESLER; *Waiter,* ALFRED NEUGEBAUER; *Men in courtroom,* EUGEN GUNTHER, KARL KNEIDINGER

As Burdach's secretary

SYNOPSIS

Because Frau Vogel, a poor flower seller, does not have enough money to pay the dog tax, officials have seized her pet. She goes to the home of Alderman Dr. Thoss to ask his help so that she may keep her dog. Having tea with Thoss's wife Victoria is Burdach, an ambitious young newspaperman. The reporter is waiting to interview Dr. Thoss about his program if he is elected mayor.

Frau Vogel tells Victoria and Burdach why she is there and immediately gains their sympathy. However, when Dr. Thoss arrives home, he ejects her from the house. He tells her that the law must take its course and that she must await its decision.

Burdach finds this most unfair and cruel. He decides to write an account of Frau Vogel's story and prints the account in the same issue of the paper that carries his inter-

An English language version of *Sturm im Wasserglas* was made and released in England in 1937, titled *Storm in a Teacup*. Vivien Leigh and Rex Harrison were the stars, and Sara Allgood played the old flower lady.

REVIEWS

VARIETY

The type of comedy this film is built on is all too rare in films. Perhaps, from a box-office standpoint, justly so. It's pathos of a clear calibre, such as is touched only by Chaplin. . . . It's handled extremely well and gets every bit possible out of the story. Hansi Niese, a fine character actress, previously seen here in unimpressive roles, turns in a splendid performance as the old flower lady. She whimpers, cries and cajoles, but never descends into bathos. . . . Renate Müller, one of the best of the German actresses, is the pretty young wife of the politician. . . . Photography and direction are good.

FILM DAILY

Hansi Niesi, comedienne in the feature, handles her substantial part in much of the Marie Dressler fashion, the result being many good laughs and a host of chuckles. . . . Direction is fine, photography good.

THE NEW YORK TIMES

Renate Müller again captivates her audience, although she is not allowed to "steal the show" from Hansi Niesi, the veteran Austrian actress who fills the title role (Blumenfrau). There is plenty of fun for those understanding German in this happy mixture of love, politics and canine interest in a provincial German town, and the action is so simple and the direction so good that even persons not familiar with the language are likely to be entertained, especially if they read the English summary in advance.

view with Dr. Thoss.

Because of the dog story, no one believes Dr. Thoss's professions of humanity, and he is laughed out of a meeting. He meets further trouble when Victoria divorces him for having an affair with a girl named Lisa.

Burdach loses his job over the incident, but he and Victoria fall in love and decide to marry. Frau Vogel's dog is returned to her; she is awarded the sum of 1,600 marks, and she marries the dog catcher.

NOTES

Sturm im Wasserglas, a film of tender emotions, was sensitively played by a cast of highly accomplished actors. This was Hedy's second film and the last in which she had a bit part, that of a secretary in a newspaper office. Heading the cast was one of Europe's top stars of the day, the lovely blonde Renate Müller, whose unfortunate indiscretion (in real life) with Adolf Hitler resulted in her downfall and death. The flower woman was splendidly portrayed by that fine character actress Hansi Niesi, who was called the Marie Dressler of Austria.

With Harald Paulsen

WIR BRAUCHEN KEIN GELD
WE NEED NO MONEY

Also known as
MAN BRAUCHT KEIN GELD
(in Germany)
HIS MAJESTY, KING BALLYHOO
(in USA)

A Sascha-Film Production   (Austrian—1931)

CREDITS

Directed by Karl Boese. *Produced by* Dr. Wilhelm Szekely. *Screenplay by* Karl Noti and Hans Wilhelm. *Based on a play by* F. Altenkirch. *Cameraman,* Willy Goldberger. *Photograph direction by* Karl Sander. *Art direction by* Julius von Borsody. *Music arranged by* Artur Guttmann. *Film editor,* G. Pollatschik. *Sound recording,* Erich Lange. *Photos by* Rudi Brix. *Running time, 87 minutes.*

CAST

Schmidt, HEINZ RÜHMANN; *Käthe Brandt,* HEDY KIESLER; *Thomas Hoffmann,* HANS MOSER; *Frau Brandt,* IDA WÜST; *Herr Brandt,* HANS JUNKERMANN; *Bank President,* KURT GERRON; *The Mayor,* PAUL HENCKELS; *with:* HANS HERMANN SCHAUFUSS, ALBERT FLORATH, LUDWIG STOESSEL, HUGO FISCHER-KÖPPE, SIEGFRIED BERISCH, WOLFGANG VON SCHWIND, HEINRICH SCHROTH, FRITZ ODEMAR, LEOPOLD VON LEDEBOUR, SIGI HOFER, KARL HANNEMANN, *and* ANNA DAMMANN

SYNOPSIS

Thomas Hoffmann, an uncle from Chicago, arrives in the little village of Groditzkirchen. He comes with only a ten-dollar gold piece in his pocket but soon is made an honorary citizen of the town.

From the time of his arrival, he sets out to bluff his way into the world of business and finance and strikes a mighty blow against the existing system of producing and distributing wealth. He does all this with such charm and grace that even the promoters and financiers, whom he holds up to scorn, can hardly be offended.

Then there is the bank clerk, Herr Schmidt; he exploits the credit theory for his own benefit, for Käthe—his sweetheart—her family, and the entire town, and in sympathy with Uncle Hoffmann, who is forced into playing the role of a millionaire in spite of his vigorous objections.

With Heinz Rühmann

As Käthe Brandt

A Vienna newspaper ad

85

With Heinz Rühmann, Ida Wüst, Hans Junkermann
and Hans Moser

Comedy, straight and unadulterated, holds the screen
with the presence of a pleasant German import pretty well
warranted to provide a good time for those who understand the language in which the nifties and witty sayings
are spoken. . . . The film is well directed and well played,
with Heinz Rühmann winning the lion's share of laurels.
Hedy Kiesler, an easy-to-look-at Viennese player, is decorative as the ingenue.

FILM DAILY

Lively comedy of German life featuring Heinz
Rühmann. . . . A pleasing little travesty on American
promotion methods that carries a lot of light-comedy
touches and amusing characterizations.

NEW YORK SUN

Well, the Germans are endeavoring to play farce again.
The result is the usual heavy-handed one. This time the
talkie is called *Wir Brauchen Kein Geld* ("His Majesty,
King Ballyhoo"). It is a typical American story of bluffing
to success—however the Berlin studios got hold of it—but
when we Americans do it with some sort of pace, bright
humor and vitality, the Germans do it with all the pace of a
funeral. . . . The acting is typically Germanic, slow and
clumsy for this sort of thing—the only bright spot of "His
Majesty, King Ballyhoo" being the general attractiveness
of a new Teutonic miss, Hedy Kiesler.

NEW YORK POST

One doesn't need to understand German to derive con-
tinuous merriment from what seems to this reviewer to be
the best comedy film that has come to us labeled "Made in
Germany". . . . The acting is uncommonly good, especially by Heinz Rühmann as Schmidt, the bank clerk;
Hans Moser as the martyred uncle from America, and
Hedy Kiesler, the girl, who neatly demonstrates that German and Austrian movie actresses need not necessarily all
be Marlene Dietrichs.

REVIEWS

THE NEW YORK TIMES

Again the Teutonic film makers prove that they can take
a well-worn subject and revamp it into a highly entertaining picture. . . . Excellent work by a cast of familiar German actors, reinforced by Hedy Kiesler, a charming Austrian girl, and fine photography and sound reproduction
make this effort thoroughly enjoyable.

NEW YORK WORLD-TELEGRAM

Like most of the German films, it boasts of good, though
in this instance by no means impressive acting. But this
acting cannot help the film out of the predicament that
confronts it, which is once again the almost total inability
of the Germans to project comedy across the screen. . . .
Heinz Rühmann is good as the ambitious bank clerk, the
role of the American relative is well managed by Hans
Moser and Hedy Kiesler makes an attractive ingenue.

NOTES

In her first starring picture, Hedy had the good fortune
to have Heinz Rühmann as her leading man. Rühmann,
who has had a long and successful career as Germany's
number-one star, is primarily known to Americans for his
role in Stanley Kramer's *Ship of Fools*. Hans Moser (*Geld
auf der Strasse*) had an amusing part in the film as the
uncle from America. A supporting role was played by
Ludwig Stoessel, who later became famous as the Little
Old Wine Maker in U.S. TV commercials.

With Heinz Rühmann

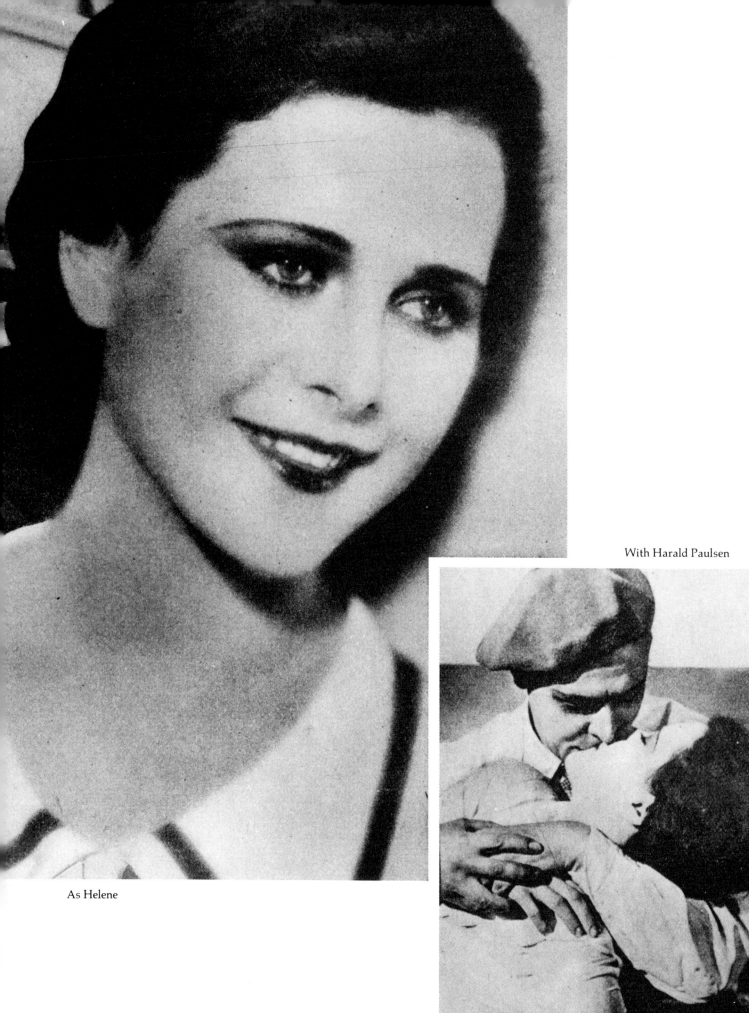

With Harald Paulsen

As Helene

DIE KOFFER DES HERRN O. F.
THE TRUNKS OF MR. O. F.

A Tobis-Film Production   (German—1932)

CREDITS

Directed by Alexis Granowsky. *Produced by* Hans Conradi *and* Mark Asarow. *Screenplay by* Leo Lania *and* Alexis Granowsky. *Based on a story by* Hans Hömberg. *Directors of photography,* Reimar Kuntze *and* Heinrich Balasch. *Sets by* Erich Czerwonsky. *Costumes by* Edward Suhr. *Music by* Dr. Karol Rathaus. *Songs by* Erich Kästner. *The songs:* "Hausse-Song"; "Cabaretsong"; "Barcarole"; "Die Kleine Ansprache"; *and* "Schluss-song". *Music conducted by* Kurt Schröder. *Assistant director,* Jakob Gartner. *Film editors,* Paul Falkenberg *and* Curt von Molo. *Sound editor,* Hans Grimm.

CAST

The Mayor, ALFRED ABEL; *Stix,* PETER LORRE; *Stark,* HARALD PAULSEN; *Helene (Mayor's daughter),* HEDY KIESLER; *Brunn,* LUDWIG STOESSEL; *Viola Volant,* MARGO LION; *Mayor's wife,* ILSE KORSECK; *Eve Lune,* LISKA MARCH; *Stark's assistant,* ARIBERT MOG; *Assistant in salon,* GABY KARPELES; *Jean (a hairdresser),* HADRIAN MARIA NETTO; *Jean's wife,* HERTHA VON WALTHER; *Dorn (a tailor),* FRANZ WEBER; *Dorn's wife,* MARIA KARSTEN; *Alexander (Helene's brother),* FRED DÖDERLEIN; *Professor Smith,* BERNHARD GOETZKE; *Jean's mother-in-law,* JOSEPHINE DORA; *A druggist,* FRIEDRICH ETTEL; *Frau Beck (a landlady),* AENNE GÖRLING; *The doctor,* MEINHARDT MAUR; *Maitre d'Hotel,* RALF OSTERMANN; *Bank director,* HENRY PLESS; *Bank director's secretary,* GERTRUD OBER; *Peter,* HANS HERMANN SCHAUFUSS; *A film producer,* R. HOFBAUER; *A film director,* ARTHUR MAINZER; *travel agent,* EDUARD ROTHAUSER

With Harald Paulsen

SYNOPSIS

Thirteen trunks marked O.F. have been sent to a quiet little German town. The trunks are delivered to the only hotel in town, accompanied by a letter stating that Mr. O.F. will arrive within a few days. Brunn, the hotel owner, has his establishment redecorated. The local stores follow suit.

Stix, the local newspaper editor, hints in his paper that Mr. O.F., owner of the trunks, is a wealthy man with plans to invest money in the town.

Several weeks pass and Mr. O.F. still has not arrived. The hotel proprietor tires of waiting for the unknown guest, and substitutes another man for him. Then he announces that Mr. O.F. is under the care of a physician and cannot receive visitors.

The townspeople become enthusiastic; a tremendous boom starts, which results in enormous building projects. The town becomes a city. By the time townspeople learn that the guest of the hotel owner is not O.F., it no longer is important whether the real O.F. existed or not, and a conference on international economics meets to establish how the city came to sudden prosperity.

REVIEWS

CLOSE UP (ENGLAND)

All that might have been thought out quite nicely, but was worked out wrongly—approximately with the means of the cabaret *Blauer Vogel*—decorative and playful, impressive and wrong. The settings are more important than the play and the idea is hidden behind beautiful paintings. This farce on the economic crisis reminds us of a juggler who appears with a serious face of a doctor at the deathbed of the patient and who promises to bring him new life. Then he begins to tickle the patient until he laughingly expires. . . . With *Die Koffer Des Herrn O.F.,* here is a statement, but it is kept secret.

THE NEW YORK TIMES

Die Koffer Des Herrn O.F. is a film that nobody should miss who is interested in the screen's future. There are moments in it in which the stylization is successful and points new paths for the screen. Particularly, the scenes that are underlined by Karol Rathaus' sensitive music I thought worth seeing again. Can I say more?

NOTES

This delightful little German comedy provided Hedy with her second role, which, as the mayor's daughter, she played with sincere charm. Ludwig Stoessel, who had been in *Wir Brauchen Kein Geld,* was impressive as the hotel owner, as was Alfred Abel as the mayor. Aribert Mog, in a minor role, later played Hedy's lover in *Ecstasy,* and Peter Lorre (the newspaper editor) was reunited with Hedy in Hollywood several years later in *The Conspirators* and *The Story of Mankind.*

Featured in the cast was Margo Lion, thinner than a Ritz cracker, who was a popular star of the Wilde Bühne carbaret in Berlin. She was the kind of girl that Christopher Isherwood described so well in his stories of that era of "divine decadence" in prewar Germany. Fräulein Lion was also the star of "Es liegt in der Luft" (It is in the Air) in the Berlin Komödie that featured an up and coming young actress named Marlene Dietrich.

With Alfred Abel

EKSTASE
ECSTASY
Also known as
SYMPHONIE DER LIEBE
SYMPHONY OF LOVE
An Elekta Film Production (Czechoslovakia —1933)

As Eva

With Jaromir Rogoz

CREDITS

Directed by Gustav Machaty. *Produced by* Franz Horky and Moriz Grünhut. *Written by* Gustav Machaty, Franz Horky, *and* Vitezslav Nezval. *'Dialogue by* Jacques A. Koerpel. *Directors of photography,* Jan Stalich *and* Hans Androschin. *Art direction by* Bohumil Hes. *Sets by* Hösch. *Music by* Dr. Josef Becce. *Music conducted by* Kopf *and* Herz. *Sound recording,* Josef Statter *and* Stal. *Running time, 82 minutes.*

CAST

Eva, HEDY KIESLER; *Emile,* JAROMIR ROGOZ; *Adam,* ARIBERT MOG; *Eva's father,* LEOPOLD KRAMER

SYNOPSIS

Eva, a young girl, marries Emile, a wealthy old man. On their wedding night, the elderly groom fussily follows his bachelor routine. Waiting for her husband to come to her, she finds he has fallen asleep.

Immediately, she has doubts about her marriage. Emile is always kind, but their relationship is not that of husband and wife.

Leaving him, Eva returns to her father's house in the country. While horseback riding by a lake one day, she impulsively stops, disrobes, ties her clothes to the saddle, and goes for a swim.

Her mare gallops off, taking her clothes along. Adam, a young engineer, suddenly appears and seizes the mare's bridle.

Eva, naked, tries to hide. Embarrassed, she crouches in the bushes as she watches Adam come nearer. She is excited by his youth and manliness, the complete opposite of her old husband.

Later that night, she goes to the young man's cabin. He makes love to her, and they formulate plans to run away together.

Returning to her father's house, Eva finds Emile waiting; he begs her to return to him. She tells him that it is too late. On his way back to town, he stops at Adam's cabin to ask for a drink. He sees Eva's pearls there and guesses that the young man is her lover.

Emile remains silent. Later, from the balcony of an inn, he watches as the lovers meet below. Heartsick, he kills himself.

Eva is horrified over what has happened. She does not tell Adam that the dead man had been her husband. Instead, they go to the railroad station and prepare to leave as planned.

Stricken with remorse, she believes that she is responsible for Emile's death. She kisses Adam, who has fallen asleep, and slips away, out of his life. For one night of ecstasy, a lifetime of sorrow ahead.

REVIEWS

WASHINGTON POST

Its highly emotional theme, exquisitely interpreted, largely in pantomine, by Hedy Kiesler, and beautifully photographed in typical European "art" manner, the picture presents what is quite the acme, to date, of symbolic artistry.

HOLLYWOOD SPECTATOR

Ecstasy can be nothing less than a great artistic experience. It is not pornographic because it does not degrade sex. It is as valid to condemn *Ecstasy* for its "erotics" as it would be to object to *A Connecticut Yankee in King Arthur's Court* because it is full of anachronisms. These qualities in each case are vital and essential to the theme. To remove them would in one instance be to render a great comedy meaningless, in the other to destroy a profoundly moving work of art.

NEW YORK HERALD TRIBUNE

Hedy Lamarr is appealing as the romantic young wife. She goes through her role thoroughly, her facial expressions are most expressive and the lack of dialogue on her part is not greatly missed. However, we did wish the other principals, Jaromir Rogoz, Leopold Kramer and Aribert Mog, had spoken more than they did—if only to relieve the monotony.

RICHMOND (VA.) NEWS LEADER

The picture has been so well acted that the few English words which have been dubbed in are superfluous and create something of a jarring note. . . . It is a pleasure to behold such excellent examples of the camera's art as the picture represents.

A frame from the film during the
moments of ecstasy

With Aribert Mog

NOTES

Director Machaty committed the same crime on film as Gustav Flaubert had done in print seventy-five years before with *Madame Bovary.* That a married woman of breeding would leave the bed of a devoted husband for another man was not only scandalous but downright criminal. Emma Bovary and Machaty's Eva, not unalike, were sisters in arms, perhaps forerunners in the cause of women's liberation.

There has been much written about *Ecstasy,* both pro and con. Called a major film achievement by many, it has been judged unimportant by others. It is a film one must see and judge for himself. If he is fortunate to see the original uncut version, then he is in for a rare film experience. But if he sees the hackneyed version pieced together by exhibitor Samuel Cummins, that is another story.

Cummins obtained the exclusive distribution rights for presenting *Ecstasy* in the United States. But due to the strict censorship code of the time, he was told that he would never get it shown. The erotic love scene between a married woman and her lover was unthinkable. However, Cummins managed to outsmart the censors and get it shown. He ingeniously accomplished the impossible by getting the lovers married before the great moment of "ecstasy." Just before that moment, a diary was introduced and across the screen were the words: "Adam and I were secretly married today." Also, just to stress the fact, a voice, supposedly Hedy's, is heard to say in measured English: "I am so lonely. I must tell father we are married."

Because it was so severely cut, Americans never got to see much of the intercourse scene that had sent Europeans sweating and panting from the theaters. A few trick shots of Hedy's facial expressions while being pawed by Mog remained, and the fingers of an outstretched hand twirling the fringe of the rug gives one a pretty good idea of what is going on. The famous swimming scene and the run through the woods were allowed to remain intact. But Cummins's print of the picture was of such poor quality that the viewing was not pleasurable.

To induce audiences into the theater, Cummins advertised the picture with such clichés as "daring" . . . "revealing" . . . "shocking"—and used such blatant phrases as: "The stark naked truth of a woman's desire for love." "A bold story of a delicate subject." "The most whispered-about picture in the world."

An illicit woman was not allowed future happiness on the screen in those days, so the final scene is not a happy one. While the couple await the train to Berlin, Mog falls asleep; Hedy kisses him and walks away. The oncoming express is seen approaching, leaving the viewer to decide for himself if Hedy steps in front of it, on it, or just walks away.

ALGIERS

A United Artists Picture (1938)

With Charles Boyer

CREDITS

Directed by John Cromwell. *Produced by* Walter Wanger. *Screenplay by* John Howard Lawson *and* James M. Cain. *Based on the book Pepe le Moko by* Detective Ashelbe. *Director of photography,* James Wong Howe. *Art direction by* Alexander Tuluboff. *Miss Lamarr's costumes by* Irene. *Wardrobe by* Omar Kiam. *Music by* Vincent Scott *and* Mohammed Igorbouchen. *Lyrics by* Ann Ronell. *Sound recording,* James Neal. *Film editors,* Otho Lovering *and* William Reynolds. *Running time, 95 minutes.*

CAST

Pepe Le Moko, CHARLES BOYER; *Gaby,* HEDY LAMARR; *Ines,* SIGRID GURIE; *Slimane,* JOSEPH CALLEIA; *Regis,* GENE LOCKHART; *Pierrot,* JOHNNY DOWNS; *Grandpere,* ALAN HALE; *Tania,* MME. NINA KOSHETZ; *Aicha,* JOAN WOODBURY; *Marie,* CLAUDIA DELL; *Giroux,* ROBERT GREIG; *Carlos,* STANLEY FIELDS; *Max,* CHARLES D. BROWN; *Gil,* BEN HALL; *L'Arbi,* LEONID KINSKY; *Louvain,* WALTER KINGSFORD; *Janvier,* PAUL HARVEY; *Maxim Bertier,* BERT ROACH; *Waitress,* LUANA WALTERS; *French Police Sergeant,* ARMAND KALIS

SYNOPSIS

Pepe Le Moko, a noted jewel thief, has fled Paris to avoid arrest. He has taken refuge in the Casbah, an impenetrable section of Algiers inhabited mainly by crooks. Pepe's morale is broken by confinement in the strange new place. He longs for France and the things he loved.

An Algerian girl, Ines, adores him but realizes that he only tolerates her. A detective, Slimane, sees Pepe every day and waits for the day when he can lure Pepe from the Casbah in order to arrest him. He is sure that Pepe's spirit eventually will break.

This happens much sooner than Slimane expects. Touring the quarter with friends is Gaby, a beautiful Parisian girl who becomes attracted to Pepe. The two fall in love. Gaby steals away from her fiance each day to meet him.

As Gaby

With Claudia Dell, Bert Roach and
Joseph Calleia

With Claudia Dell, Robert Greig
(behind Hedy) and Bert Roach

It is through Gaby and his love for her that Pepe realizes how much he loves Paris and what he is missing. He becomes more depressed.

Gaby is led to believe that Pepe has been killed and decides to leave Algiers and return to Paris at once. Pepe sneaks out of the Casbah and buys a ticket on the same steamer to France. Ines, unable to bear his leaving her, informs the police.

As he is taken off the boat, Pepe sees Gaby and runs toward her. Thinking he is trying to escape, one of the detectives shoots him. Pepe dies, and Gaby leaves for Paris alone.

With Joseph Calleia, Ben Hall, Joan Woodbury, Charles D. Brown and Charles Boyer

With Joseph Calleia

REVIEWS

NEW YORK HERALD TRIBUNE

The performing is uniformly fine. Hedy Lamarr, famous as the leading woman in *Ecstasy,* brings rare beauty and talent to her first American assignment as the girl who unwittingly lures Pepe into the hands of the police.

NEW YORK WORLD-TELEGRAM

Crime and punishment the Algerian way. Excellent. Even without the presence of the dazzling Hedy Lamarr in its cast, *Algiers* would still be a tasty dish. . . . Hedy Lamarr gives a vivid and forthright performance. But whether she is a good actress or not will make practically no difference at all once you get an eyeful of her brunette beauty. It's exactly what the doctor ordered in the way of glamour, and for once the west coast critics weren't exaggerating when they called her a knockout.

VARIETY

Other meritorious aspects include John Cromwell's direction and the first appearance in an American film of Hedy Lamarr, the alluring natatorial star of the much censored *Ecstasy*. Playing the leading feminine role opposite Boyer, she brings an abundance of good looks, acting talent and enticement. Considering that all her previous performances have been in foreign-made pictures, her English diction is clear and distinct, and nothing apparently stands between her and success in Hollywood films.

PHOTOPLAY

Boyer is superb. Gene Lockhart, as the informer, does the finest characterization of his career. But it's delicious, dark-eyed Hedy Lamarr, making her American debut, who steals her every scene by the sheer lovely sex she exudes.

NOTES

Producer Walter Wanger was so impressed with the French film *Pepe le Moko,* which was directed by Julien Duvivier and starred Jean Gabin, that he arranged to buy the rights to the story as a starring vehicle for Charles Boyer.

James M. Cain and John Howard Lawson translated the French into English and changed the title to *Algiers,* which John Cromwell directed nearly scene for scene from the original.

Dolores Del Rio was originally scheduled to play Gaby, the French adventuress, but a satisfactory deal could not be made. Wanger tried next to get Sylvia Sidney for the part, but she was not interested. She neither liked Hollywood nor making pictures and turned down the offer in favor of the Broadway stage.

Through a chance meeting, Boyer met Hedy Lamarr and insisted that no one but she should play Gaby. Hedy was sitting around MGM waiting for a picture when Wanger bargained for her services. Her American debut was so sensational that she became an international star overnight. Boyer was so enthralled by her that he seemed to be half embalmed throughout the picture and didn't seem to care that her mere presence knocked him clear off the screen.

"Come wiz me to the Casbah" is a phrase assumed by many as having been spoken to Hedy by Boyer. Due to the popularity of the film, many Boyer mimics used that phrase in their acts even though it was never spoken in the film. It couldn't have been, since Boyer was already in the Casbah and never left until the end of the film.

Algiers, although a bit slow moving at times, especially when Hedy is not on screen, is a well-mounted film. Alexander Tuluboff's recreation of the Casbah is so real that one almost believes the picture was filmed on location. Another asset is the artistry of James Wong Howe's camera. Both Tuluboff and Howe received Academy Award nominations for their fine work.

Universal-International bought the rights to the story from Wanger in 1948 and called their remake *Casbah,* which turned out to be a pale imitation of its predecessor. Tony Martin was a poor choice for Pepe, and Yvonne De-Carlo was only adequate as Ines. Peter Lorre as Slimane was good but not better than Joseph Calleia. Those who remembered Hedy Lamarr's fabulous Gaby of ten years before could not accept Marta Toren in the role.

With Robert Taylor

LADY OF THE TROPICS
A Metro-Goldwyn-Mayer Picture (1939)

CREDITS

Directed by Jack Conway. *Produced by* Sam Zimbalist. *Screenplay by* Ben Hecht. *Director of photography,* George Folsey. *Art direction by* Cedric Gibbons *and* Paul Groesse. *Set decoration by* Edwin B. Willis. *Gowns by* Adrian. *Men's costumes by* Valles. *Music by* Franz Waxman. *Song,* "Each Time You Say Goodbye (I Die a Little)," *by* Phil Ohlman *and* Foster Carlin. *Film editor,* Elmo Vernon. *Running time, 91 minutes.*

CAST

Bill Carey, ROBERT TAYLOR; *Manon de Vargnes,* HEDY LAMARR; *Pierre Delaroch,* JOSEPH SCHILD-KRAUT; *Nina,* GLORIA FRANKLIN; *Father Antoine,* ERNEST COSSART; *Dolly Harrison,* MARY TAYLOR; *Alfred Z. Harrison,* CHARLES TROWBRIDGE; *Colonel Demassey,* FREDERICK WORLOCK; *Lamartine,* PAUL PORCASI; *Madame Kya,* MARGARET PADULA; *Countess Berichi,* CECIL CUNNINGHAM; *Mrs. Hazlitt,* NATALIE MOORHEAD

SYNOPSIS

Playboy Bill Carey, visiting with his fiancee and her family, in French Indo-China, meets Manon de Vargnes, a beautiful half-caste girl, and they fall in love and marry.

Through Pierre Delaroch, a wealthy and influential man and himself a Eurasian, Manon hopes to obtain a passport so that she may leave the Orient with her husband. Delaroch, also in love with her, stalls the issuance of the passport.

Bill cannot find a job, and their money runs out. Manon promises herself to Delaroch if he will give Bill work and get her a passport. Delaroch agrees and sends an unsuspecting Bill to work on a rubber plantation in the jungle.

When Bill returns, Delaroch leads him to believe that Manon has been unfaithful. He vows to kill Delaroch. Having done nothing more than attend an opera with Delaroch, Manon reaches Delaroch first, kills him, then shoots herself. Bill finds her and forgives her. But it is too late. Manon dies clutching the passport she has finally acquired.

As Manon de Vargnes

106

With Joseph Schildkraut

With Robert Taylor

REVIEWS

NEW YORK HERALD TRIBUNE

Lady of the Tropics is important because it marks the first appearance together of Miss Hedy Lamarr and Robert Taylor, two of the screen's most glamorous figures. *Lady of the Tropics* starts out to be quite dull. But that is before Miss Lamarr begins to work. The secret of her fascination lies in her face, her features and her eyes. She can look like a Madonna; she can wrench one's heart with pity, with animation or any other of physical or mental expression. While her voice is by no means equal to her other equipment, it is pleasing, and she uses it often and to good advantage in the film.

HOLLYWOOD REPORTER

M-G-M has a terrific attraction in *Lady of the Tropics* because M-G-M has Hedy Lamarr—and has her in the picture. Nothing else seemed to matter to this reviewer last night in watching the preview of the picture. True, Bob Taylor, quite a star in his own right, was in the picture and certainly M-G-M and Sam Zimbalist gave it fine production, with a Ben Hecht script and other trimmings to attractively mount that beautiful woman. All of it meant little in our final estimation compared to Hedy. She is the star, she is the great attraction, she is the entertainment. . . . The important thing is Hedy Lamarr. Her millions of fans will rave over the picture because she is in almost every scene and gives an excellent performance.

NEW YORK DAILY NEWS

About the only lasting impression that *Lady of the Tropics* will make on you is Hedy Lamarr, Ed Sullivan's entry in the race for the most beautiful woman of all times. . . . She is so lovely in this picture that you'll probably forget that the story, cooked up by Ben Hecht for the special occasion of presenting Metro-Goldwyn-Mayer's star to the public that has awaited her appearance since *Algiers*, was a sentimental affair that moved along at a pedestrian pace. . . . There's little else to say, good or bad, about the new picture, except that it is worth taking a look at just to see Hedy Lamarr. And you really will come away trying to recall one more beautiful.

Robert Taylor and Hedy Lamarr, the latter appearing to much greater advantage than in any of her previous appearances and oozing glamour at every turn, are splendid in a screenplay, which despite certain obvious weaknesses is beautifully molded to their joint talents as screen lovers, the joining of whom is sure to have general fan approval.

Lady of the Tropics has Hedy Lamarr . . . more beautiful, more glamorous than anyone who has ever hit the screen. MGM wisely realized that the first requisite was photographing this asset to the best advantage and to George Folsey, A.S.C., was given this task, which he performs admirably.

NOTES

Lady of the Tropics can be cited as one of those cases in which the actress rises above the material. Ben Hecht's script wasn't up to his usual high quality, nor was Jack Conway's overall direction. Also, Robert Taylor, as the weak husband, although handsome, was of no support, and his acting was one-dimensional. But Hedy's touching performance as the tragic Eurasian girl, enhanced greatly by George Folsey's masterful camera work, was one of her best.

Because the team of Lamarr and Taylor met with such great favor with the public, MGM decided to co-star the two in another film. A screenplay by Walter Reisch and Samuel Hoffenstein called *Guns and Fiddles* was decided on, and the singer Miliza Korjus, who had appeared in Metro's *The Great Waltz,* was assigned the third starring role. However, by the time shooting could get under way, filming was reactivated on *I Take This Woman* and Hedy was put to work in that. In the meantime, she wangled herself one of the leading roles in *Boom Town,* and the Lamarr-Taylor project was dropped.

I TAKE THIS WOMAN

A Metro-Goldwyn-Mayer Picture   (1940)

CREDITS

Directed by W. S. Van Dyke II. *Screenplay by* James Kevin McGuinness. *Original story by* Charles MacArthur. *Director of photography,* Harold Rosson. *Art direction by* Cedric Gibbons *and* Paul Groesse. *Gowns by* Adrian. *Music by* Bronislau Kaper. *Recording director,* Douglas Shearer. *Film editor,* George Boemler. *Running time, 96 minutes.*

CAST

Karl Decker, SPENCER TRACY; *Georgi Gragore,* HEDY LAMARR; *Madame Maresca,* VERREE TEASDALE; *Phil Mayberry,* KENT TAYLOR; *Linda Rodgers,* LARAINE DAY; *Sandra Mayberry,* MONA BARRIE; *Joe,* JACK CARSON; *Bill Rodgers,* PAUL CAVANAGH; *Dr. Duveen,* LOUIS CALHERN; *Lola Estermonte,* FRANCES DRAKE; *Gertie,* MARJORIE MAIN; *Joe Barnes,* DALIES FRANTZ; *Bob Hampton,* REED HADLEY; *Katz,* GEORGE E. STONE; *Sambo,* WILLIE BEST; *Pancho,* LEON BELASCO; *Ted Fenton,* DON CASTLE; *Dr. Morris,* CHARLES TROWBRIDGE; *Lt. of Police,* CHARLES D. BROWN; *Butler,* LOWDEN ADAMS; *Dr. Phelps,* GAYNE WHITMAN; *Intern,* JOHN SHELTON; *Intern,* TOM COLLINS; *Mrs. Bettincourt,* FLORENCE SHIRLEY; *Raoul Cedro,* RAFAEL STORM; *Saleslady,* NATALIE MOORHEAD

As Georgi Gragore

SYNOPSIS

Karl Decker, a doctor sailing back to America after doing research work abroad, prevents Georgi Gragore from committing suicide. She has had a disappointing love affair with Phil Mayberry, who has promised to divorce his wife and marry her. But Phil changed his mind and returned to the United States.

Karl suggests to Georgi that she give up her job in the fashion business and find some serious work to do. Following his advice, she asks him to let her work in his clinic in a poor tenement district.

Karl falls in love with her, and she accepts his marriage proposal. But even after marriage, she cannot forget Phil. Karl, eager to give his wife luxuries, leaves the clinic and becomes a society doctor.

Georgi, after a visit to Phil, finally realizes that she loves her husband. Overjoyed, she makes plans for a second honeymoon. Karl finds out about her visit to Phil and decides to break up the marriage.

Karl is called to the hospital, where he learns that a case has been bungled by a young intern. The man's career will be ruined.

Not caring what happens anymore, Karl takes the blame. He goes to the clinic to bid farewell and finds Georgi there.

The mistake at the hospital is cleared up, and he realizes that his place is at the clinic—and with Georgi.

REVIEWS

VARIETY

Story flounders with numerous uninteresting passages that are lifted somewhat by persuasive performances of both Tracy and Miss Lamarr. Situations are not too clearly defined, and in several spots lengthy dialogue sequences prove tiresome. . . . Tracy and Miss Lamarr do nobly under trying conditions.

NEW YORK DAILY WORKER

Somebody at MGM heard that the day of the glamorous screen siren is over. The trend of the times is toward actresses who can act. And so Hedy Lamarr is given a vehicle in which to prove that she can do more than wear lipstick. The result is called *I Take This Woman* and is the most bewildering bad film that has come in a couple of very lean months. It isn't Miss Lamarr's fault, either. It turns out she isn't all lethargy and languor after all. It's even possible that she might be a completely charming light comedienne. But not in this script. Better actors than

With Dalies Frantz, Don Castle,
Tom Collins, Spencer Tracy and
John Shelton

With Spencer Tracy and Verree
Teasdale

With Spencer Tracy and Louis Calhern

With Spencer Tracy, Kent Taylor, Laraine Day, Paul Cavanagh, Frances Drake and Reed Hadley

she go down in these seas, and without the costumes she has to drag her down. . . . The only important thing about *I Take This Woman* is that it was given as an assignment to serious, self-respecting artists. And things being as they are in Hollywood, they probably had to take it. . . .

NEW YORK DAILY MIRROR

The one-woman-beauty-trust came to the Music Hall yesterday starred in that rarest of curios, a picture better than its advance notices. . . . Spencer Tracy fans will be delighted by his performance. Everyone will be delighted by Hedy Lamarr. But why must script writers fall in love with their own words?

NEW YORK DAILY NEWS

Hedy is given a terrific build-up in the picture, a build-up that would faze a more experienced actress than Miss Lamarr pretends to be. . . .

Hedy holds the attention of Frank Borzage, Spencer
Tracy and Robert Taylor (visiting the set) during the
filming. Borzage was one of several directors who
worked on the picture

With Kent Taylor and Mona Barrie

NOTES

While in original production, this project had the working
title *A New York Cinderella.* Everyone knew this was
Metro's "Hedy Lamarr picture," the one to launch her
American career. This did not please Spencer Tracy, who
felt his talents were being used to beef up a picture that
would bring plenty of publicity for Hedy and none for him.

He shouldn't have worried. The final result was a disas-
ter and did not help Hedy one bit. The production ran into
so much trouble that it was shut down after director Josef
von Sternberg quit because of set interference by Louis B.
Mayer.

Under the new title, *I Take This Woman,* with W. S.
Van Dyke at the helm, production resumed over a year
later. So much footage was shot, scrapped, and shot again
that everyone began calling it *I Re-Take This Woman.*

With Spencer Tracy and Walter Pidgeon in a scene from
the original scrapped version

With Spencer Tracy

BOOM TOWN
A Metro-Goldwyn-Mayer Picture   (1940)

CREDITS

Directed by Jack Conway. *Produced by* Sam Zimbalist. *Screenplay by* John Lee Mahin. *Based on a story by* James Edward Grant. *Director of photography,* Harold Rosson. *Art direction by* Cedric Gibbons and Eddie Imazu. *Set decoration by* Edwin B. Willis. *Gowns by* Adrian. *Men's wardrobe by* Gile Steele. *Hair styles by* Sydney Guilaroff. *Music by* Franz Waxman. *Recording director,* Douglas Shearer. *Film editor,* Blanche Sewell. *Running time, 116 minutes.*

CAST

Big John McMasters, CLARK GABLE; *Square John Sand,* SPENCER TRACY; *Betsy Bartlett,* CLAUDETTE COLBERT; *Karen Vanmeer,* HEDY LAMARR; *Luther Aldrich,* FRANK MORGAN; *Harry Compton,* LIONEL ATWILL; *Harmony Jones,* CHILL WILLS; *Whitey,* MARION MARTIN; *Spanish Eva,* MINNA GOMBELL; *Ed Murphy,* JOE YULE; *Tom Murphy,* HORACE MURPHY; *McCreery,* RAY GORDON; *Assistant District Attorney,* RICHARD LANE; *Little Jack,* CASEY JOHNSON; *Baby Jack,* BABY QUINTANILLA; *Judge,* GEORGE LESSEY; *Miss 'Barnes,* SARA HADEN; *Barber,* FRANK ORTH; *Deacon,* FRANK McGLYNN, SR.; *Ferdie,* CURT BOIS

SYNOPSIS

John McMasters and John Sand, two wildcat oil drillers, become partners and bring in a well that makes them rich. McMasters goes to town to celebrate, leaving Sand at the field to write to his girl back home, whom he plans to marry. In town, McMasters meets Betsy Bartlett; it is love at first sight for both of them, and they get married that same night. The next day, McMasters discovers that Betsy

As Karen Vanmeer

With Curt Bois, Spencer Tracy and Clark Gable

is Sand's girl. Sand is at first infuriated; but he forgives them, and the three remain good friends.

Sand finds McMasters carousing with a girl in a saloon on his first wedding anniversary and berates him. They break their friendship and flip a coin for complete ownership of the property. Sand wins.

In a short time, McMasters prospers again. He decides to branch out in the oil refinery business and to make New York his headquarters. He soon becomes acquainted with beautiful Karen Vanmeer, a girl with a past, and the two become lovers.

Sand arrives in New York; the friends become reconciled. But when Sand learns of Betsy's unhappiness, he decides to bring McMasters to his senses by ruining him financially; but Sand is ruined instead.

The government steps in; it brings an antitrust suit against McMasters. Sand comes to his support; his testimony is responsible for a dismissal of the suit.

Realizing that McMasters still loves his wife, Karen bows out. McMasters and Sand, both broke but reunited, and Betsy go west again for another wildcat adventure.

REVIEWS

VARIETY

Stars and story fit hand-and-glove. Top stars in marquee parade, Clark Gable, Spencer Tracy, Claudette Colbert, Hedy Lamarr, are not in for ornament. Each has a solid dramatic role in the burly melodrama of wildcat days and wildcat ways in development of American oil fields. None has had a better part to display individual talent and personal appeal. . . . Hedy Lamarr will be applauded for her excellent insinuating role as the smart New York girl who starts to warn Gable of his dangers from rival big operators and remains to engage his excess romantic ardor.

NEW YORK POST

In its way, the film's first half is complete in itself—the real reason for the next several reels being the introduction of the beauteous Hedy who does very capably with her siren role. Tracy and Gable are about on par for acting honors—both swell; and Miss Colbert contributes a charming account of a wife who can take it.

With Spencer Tracy,
Claudette Colbert and Clark Gable

121

With Clark Gable

NOTES

Boom Town, one of the most popular films of 1940, showed up on most of the ten-best lists of the year and was a big box-office success not only in its initial release but in subsequent reissues as well.

Hedy liked working with Gable, who became one of her two favorite leading men—James Stewart was the other—and she admired Claudette Colbert, whom she calls "a really lovely person." But Tracy was another matter. She found working with him an ordeal and was happy after each of their scenes together was completed.

Boom Town is a long picture but one that sustains interest until the end, due to James Edward Grant's fast-paced screenplay. The production is further enhanced by Harold Rosson's outstanding photography which garnered him an Academy Award nomination. The MGM special effects department, responsible for the believability of gushing oil wells and the devastation of an oil field engulfed in fire, was also Oscar-nominated.

With Clark Gable, Spencer Tracy and Claudette Colbert

With Lionel Atwill and Clark Gable

COMRADE X

A Metro-Goldwyn-Mayer Picture   (1940)

CREDITS

Directed by King Vidor. *Produced by* Gottfried Reinhardt. *Screenplay by* Ben Hecht *and* Charles Lederer. *Original story by* Walter Reisch. *Director of photography,* Joseph Ruttenberg. *Art direction by* Cedric Gibbons. *Set decoration by* Edwin B. Willis. *Women's costumes by* Adrian. *Men's clothes by* Gile Steele. *Music by* Bronislau Kaper. *Recording director,* Douglas Shearer. *Makeup by* Jack Dawn. *Film editor,* Harold F. Kress. *Running time, 90 minutes.*

CAST

McKinley B. Thompson, CLARK GABLE; *Theodore,* HEDY LAMARR; *Vasiliev,* OSCAR HOMOLKA; *Vanya,* FELIX BRESSART; *Jane Wilson,* EVE ARDEN; *Emil Von Hofer,* SIG RUMANN; *Olga,* NATASHA LYTESS; *Michael Bastakoff,* VLADIMIR SOKOLOFF; *Rubick,* EDGAR BARRIER; *Laszlo,* GEORGE RENEVANT; *Russian Officer,* MIKHAIL RASUMNY

SYNOPSIS

Vasiliev, chief of the Soviet secret police, informs foreign newspaper correspondents that until the identity of the reporter, known only as "Comrade X," who has been sending out disparaging news reports about Russia, is discovered, all news reports will be censored by him.

Vanya, a porter, discovers that McKinley B. Thompson, an American, is "Comrade X." He threatens to expose Thompson unless Thompson agrees to help his daughter Theodore, a streetcar conductor, out of the country.

Vanya fears that since Theodore is a Communist with ideals, she will be executed. Thompson meets Theodore and leads her to believe that he is a Communist; she marries him, intending to go to America to work for the party.

She soon learns that he has lied and intends to hand him over to the police. But before she can do so, the police jail her, her father, and Thompson; he has used a secret camera, and the police have found it in Vanya's room.

Sending word to Vasiliev that he has taken a picture of the man who tried to assassinate him, Thompson is taken to the police chief but finds that Vasiliev has been liquidated. Thompson finally outwits the police and escapes across the border with Theodore and Vanya in a tank they have stolen.

With Natasha Lytess

As Theodore

With Clark Gable   With Clark Gable, Felix Bressart and Oscar Homolka   With her Comrades

REVIEWS

PHILADELPHIA RECORD

Hedy is the news of the opus. Until *Comrade X,* the camera was concerned only with her bewitching beauty—which, of course, is enough. But now it seems that the lady also can act—and with a lusty sense of comedy too.

HOLLYWOOD REPORTER

The surprise of the picture is Hedy Lamarr. This gal has found herself or better, M-G-M has found her for M-G-M, for she simply knocks over her role of Theodore, looks ravishing and is the top ingredient of the show.

NEW YORK HERALD TRIBUNE

The stars are the show in the production. . . . Miss Lamarr is extremely good as the Russian girl.

SHOWMEN'S TRADE REVIEW

In this gay satire, the casting is particularly outstanding because not only is Clark Gable excellent, but Hedy Lamarr is given an opportunity to really prove her ability.

FILM DAILY

From the foreword to the finale, this new Metro offering is packed with laughs and funny situations. . . . Miss Lamarr essays a comedy role with swell results. Her acting talents assume a new sature and she definitely proves her ability as a comedienne.

NOTES

The handsome combination of Gable and Lamarr proved to be so extraordinarily appealing in *Boom Town* that Metro cast the two immediately in *Comrade X,* a lively farce sprightly directed by King Vidor.

A couple of Hedy's first films in Europe were comedies, but this was the first time in Hollywood she had the chance to prove her knack with it, which she believed was where her capabilities lay. Anyone will agree after seeing her talent for it in this picture.

The capricious screenplay by Ben Hecht and Charles Lederer was based on Walter Reisch's Academy Award-nominated original story. Reisch had been a co-author of *Ninotchka,* which had a similar plot and starred Greta Garbo the year before. Hecht also wrote a screenplay of the like sixteen years later called *The Iron Petticoat,* a Katharine Hepburn starrer.

With Clark Gable and Eve Arden

With James Stewart

COME LIVE WITH ME

A Metro-Goldwyn-Mayer Picture   (1941)

CREDITS

Produced and directed by Clarence Brown. *Screenplay by* Patterson McNutt. *Original story by* Virginia Van Upp. *Director of photography,* George Folsey. *Art direction by* Cedric Gibbons. *Set decoration by* Edwin B. Willis. *Gowns by* Adrian. *Music by* Herbert Stothart. *Recording director,* Douglas Shearer. *Film editor,* Frank E. Hull. *Running time, 85 minutes.*

CAST

Bill Smith, JAMES STEWART; *Johnny Jones,* HEDY LAMARR; *Barton Kendrick,* IAN HUNTER; *Diana Kendrick,* VERREE TEASDALE; *Joe Darsie,* DONALD MEEK; *Barney Grogan,* BARTON MacLANE; *Arnold Stafford,* EDWARD ASHLEY; *Yvonne,* ANN CODEE; *Doorman,* KING BAGGOT; *Grandma,* ADELINE DE WALT REYNOLDS; *Jerry,* FRANK ORTH; *Waiter,* FRANK FAYLEN; *Taxi Driver,* HORACE McMAHON; *Frieda,* GRETA MEYER; *Farm Hand,* SI JENKS; *Chef,* DEWEY ROBINSON; *Headwaiter,* FRITZ FELD; *Sleeping Neighbor,* JOE YULE; *Hired Hand,* TOM FADDEN; *Waiter,* GEORGE WATTS

As Johnny Jones

With Barton MacLane and Ian Hunter

With James Stewart, Dewey Robinson and Frank Faylen

SYNOPSIS

A lovely refugee, Johanna Janns, has arrived in America. Johnny, as she calls herself, is having an affair with publisher Barton Kendrick, who maintains a "modern" marriage with his wife Diana: Kendrick goes his way and Diana hers, and no questions asked.

Learning that she is to be deported, Johnny arranges to marry Bill Smith, a writer. He is broke, and Johnny agrees to pay him if he will marry her. They marry, and she takes a check to him each week. Part of the agreement is that he is not to know where she lives.

Bill is fascinated and uses it as a plot for a story. The manuscript is sent to Kendrick, who recognizes it as Johnny's story. Kendrick buys the book and advances Bill a check. Meanwhile, Johnny has started plans to marry Kendrick and serves Bill with divorce papers. Johnny's address is on the papers. Bill decides to call on her.

He asks her to spend a weekend with him on a farm; only then will he consent to a divorce. She telephones Kendrick to follow them. As the day progresses, Johnny realizes that she loves Bill.

When Kendrick shows up, Bill thinks he has come about the book. But it is not long before he guesses that Kendrick is the other man in Johnny's life. Bill leaves the house in anger.

Johnny tells Kendrick that she has decided to remain with Bill, that she really loves him. She is waiting for Bill when he returns to the house.

REVIEWS

VARIETY

Story also gives Director Brown plenty of leeway in bringing Miss Lamarr close to her full capacities as a skillful mistress of whimsy—as an actress of fine capabilities—as well as an alluring personality.

NEW YORK DAILY NEWS

The doubters will be converted after seeing Hedy Lamarr in this picture. In *Comrade X* she was all right but that role didn't call for any great display of emotion. Here, she takes off that glamorous mask and, more beautiful than ever, gives a touching performance with all the varying facial expressions necessary to make her characterization sympathetic and human. Her speaking voice has improved, also. It is no longer monotonous but rich and flexible.

RICHMOND (VA.) NEWS LEADER

While you are looking at *Come Live With Me,* you'll be aware of its evanescence, but when it's over you'll know you've been entertained. It is flimsy and charming as one of Hedy Lamarr's negligees and full of personality as James Stewart's pout, but it's entertainment and plenty of it.

PHILADELPHIA RECORD

Hedy Lamarr is beautiful. Stop. That's how a telegraphed review of *Come Live With Me* might read. Those who can look past the lovely Hedy will discover a sophisticated, amusing, romantic comedy with more than usual subtlety and not quite enough plot to last a whole movie. . . Although *Come Live With Me* falls into stock patterns, it has an easy and sophisticated charm. Miss Lamarr's luminous presence provides an extra fillip, especially when she tilts her piquant profile and rolls her liquid eyes.

A paper sculpture of Hedy and James Stewart by M-G-M publicity artist Jacques Kapralik

HOLLYWOOD REPORTER

Come Live With Me is the type of picture that every kind of audience will go for. Its romance will excite both young and old, because they both will pull for Jimmy and Hedy and root them through every situation until the final fadeout. The girls, whether daughters, mothers, or grandmothers, will go for Mr. Stewart in this new role, and the boys of any age will delight themselves with Miss Lamarr, as this is easily her best performance. Certainly she has never looked better than under the careful direction of Clarence Brown, the expert photography of George Folsey and the magnificent gowns of Adrian.

With Ian Hunter, Adeline De Walt Reynolds and James Stewart

NOTES

Come Live With Me is a cute little picture that was not intended to do any more than cash in on the popularity of the two principal players. The pair liked each other immensely and became fast friends, which made for harmonious and ideal working conditions on the set.

Hedy and Stewart were not required to do much more than play themselves in a plot that has Hedy in such desperate need to marry in order to avoid deportation that she will pay someone to marry her. As if anyone needed to be paid to marry a "dish" like that!

ZIEGFELD GIRL

A Metro-Goldwyn-Mayer Picture   (1941)

CREDITS

Directed by Robert Z. Leonard. *Produced by* Pandro S. Berman. *Screenplay by* Marguerite Roberts *and* Sonya Levien. *Written by* William Anthony McGuire. *Director of photography,* Ray June. *Art direction by* Cedric Gibbons *and* Daniel B. Cathcart. *Set decoration by* Edwin B. Willis. *Costumes by* Adrian. *Makeup by* Jack Dawn. *Recording director,* Douglas Shearer. *Film editor,* Blanche Sewell. *Musical numbers directed by* Busby Berkeley. *Music score by* Herbert Stothart. *Musical direction by* Georgie Stoll. *Vocal arrangements and orchestrations by* Leo Arnaud, George Bassman, *and* Conrad Salinger. **Songs:** *"You Stepped Out of a Dream" by* Gus Kahn *and* Nacio Herb Brown; *"Whispering" by* John Schonberger, Richard Coburn, *and* Vincent Rose; *"Mr. Gallagher and Mr. Shean" by* Ed Gallagher *and* Al Shean; *"I'm Always Chasing Rainbows" by* Joseph McCarthy *and* Harry Carroll; *"Minnie from Trinidad," "Ziegfeld Girls," and "Laugh? I Thought I'd Split My Sides" by* Roger Edens; *"Caribbean Love Song" by* Ralph Freed *and* Roger Edens; *"You Never Looked So Beautiful Before" by* Walter Donaldson (*from The Great Ziegfeld, 1936*); *"You Gotta Pull Strings" by* Harold Adamson *and* Walter Donaldson. *Running time, 135 minutes.*

CAST

Gilbert Young, JAMES STEWART; *Susan Gallagher,* JUDY GARLAND; *Sandra Kolter,* HEDY LAMARR; *Sheila Regan,* LANA TURNER; *Frank Merton,* TONY MARTIN; *Jerry Regan,* JACKIE COOPER; *Geoffrey Collis,* IAN HUNTER; *"Pop" Gallagher,* CHARLES WINNINGER; *Noble Sage,* EDWARD EVERETT HORTON; *Franz Kolter,* PHILIP DORN; *John Slayton,* PAUL KELLY; *Patsy Dixon,* EVE ARDEN; *Jimmy Walters,* DAN DAILEY, JR.; *Al,* AL SHEAN; *Mrs. Regan,* FAY

As Sandra Kolter

With Lana Turner and Judy Garland

HOLDEN; *Mischa,* FELIX BRESSART; *Mrs. Merton,* ROSE HOBART; *Nick Capalini,* BERNARD NEDELL; *Mr. Regan,* ED McNAMARA; *Jenny,* MAE BUSCH; *Annie,* RENIE RIANO; *Miss Sawyer,* JOYCE COMPTON; *Betty Regan,* RUTH TOBEY; *Native Dancer,* SERGIO ORTA; *Specialty Dancers,* ANTONIO and ROSARIO; *Geoffrey's Friend,* REED HADLEY; *Casino Patron,* BESS FLOWERS; *Pierre,* ARMAND KALIZ; *Ziegfeld Girls,* GEORGIA CARROLL, JEAN WALLACE, MYRNA DELL, CLAIRE JAMES, MADELEINE MARTIN, HARRIET BENNETT, LORRAINE GETTMAN (Leslie Brooks), VIVIEN MASON, PATRICIA DANE, LOUISE LA PLANCHE, NINA BISSELL, VIRGINIA CRUZON, ANYA TARANDA, FRANCES GLADWIN, ALAINE BRANDEIS, IRMA WILSON

With Edward Everett Horton, Lana
Turner and Eve Arden

With Edward Everett Horton and
Tony Martin

With Philip Dorn and Lana Turner

With Judy Garland and
Lana Turner

With Lana Turner, Tony Martin
Judy Garland

With Judy Garland

With Rose Hobart

SYNOPSIS

Sandra Kolter, beautiful wife of a poor violinist; Susan Gallagher, a young vaudevillian; and Sheila Regan, a pretty elevator operator, all meet at Ziegfeld's theater. They are but three girls selected to become glorified Ziegfeld girls.

Becoming a Ziegfeld girl brings fame and attention. Sandra decides to leave her husband because she thinks he doesn't believe she really loves him. Sheila develops expensive tastes and breaks up with her boy friend, Gil Young, a truck driver.

Frank Merton, the male singing star of the show, becomes attracted to the gorgeous Sandra, and the two become a steady pair. But Sandra, realizing that she could never love Frank, soon quits the show and goes back to her husband, who finally has made it as a concert violinist.

One night, Sheila goes on a drunk and is fired from the Follies. Desperately ill, she returns to her family in Brooklyn. Gil also has returned. He has been serving a jail term for bootlegging. It had seemed to him the only way to make enough money to buy Sheila the luxuries she desired so much. The two reconcile and make plans to marry.

A new Follies is about to open, and Sheila cannot bear to miss the opening. Also attending are Sandra and her husband, who are happily reconciled. Susan is the star of the show. Singing her wonderful song, she walks down the great Ziegfeld staircase just as Sandra and Sheila used to do.

Sheila cannot stand it! She leaves her seat and collapses. Sensing something wrong, Sandra comes to help. But it is too late for Sheila.

Sheila tries to speak to Sandra, but her voice fails her. From the distance, Susan's singing can be heard, and the music swells into the grand finale.

REVIEWS

CLEVELAND PRESS

Ziegfeld Girl is enormous, opulent, cost a million dollars and is very probably exactly what a good many people are looking for at the moment. Here, in other words, is escape in capital letters, garnished with tunes, glamour, beautiful young women and just about all the players on the MGM lot who weren't otherwise occupied at the time. . . . Judy Garland is more than persuasive, Lana Turner—and I couldn't have been more surprised—actually does some effective acting and anyone who doesn't believe Hedy Lamarr is one of the most beautiful women alive better go see a doctor.

With Tony Martin

With Edward Everett Horton, Eve Arden and Lana Turner

With Felix Bressart and Philip Dorn

With Lana Turner, Judy Garland and Ziegfeld girls: Virginia Cruzon, Georgia Carroll, Irma Wilson, Nina Bissell, Lorraine Gettman (Leslie Brooks), Harriet Bennett, Madeleine Martin, Anya Taranda, Patricia Dane and Alaine Brandeis

NOTES

As Ziegfeld glorifies the American girl, so does Hollywood glorify the American musical. The Ziegfeld tradition did not die with its originator. . . . *Ziegfeld Girl* is entertainment for almost every one. Even its musical moments are part of the story, not the best part, but all part of a really good show. . . . The women, of course, have all the best of it in the picture. Miss Garland, at her best when she is not being glorified, is her usual sympathetic self, singing occasionally and bringing some humor into the film. Miss Lamarr's smoldering beauty is well photographed. Miss Turner carries most of the story, as hers is the tragic tale. It is a good part and most effectively played. . . . *Ziegfeld Girl* is one of the best of the backstage pictures.

PHILADELPHIA EVENING PUBLIC LEDGER

The film is like a Ziegfeld Follies—here it's good; here it's dull. . . . As for Miss Lamarr—well, she remains histrionically unobtrusive but she really looks like the most Ziegfeldian showgirl of the lot.

MOTION PICTURE DAILY

Here is an opulent, eye-filling spectacle in the true tradition of Florenz Ziegfeld, the great spectacle-maker, and at the same time possessed of a heart-catching, human story of real people, the whole adding up to what should be box-office appeal of the widest kind and of a high order. . . . The cast is a star-studded marquee dream. The names include James Stewart, Judy Garland, Hedy Lamarr, Lana Turner, Tony Martin, Jackie Cooper, Ian Hunter, Charles Winninger, Edward Everett Horton and Paul Kelly. All give skillful performances. . . . Interspersed in the track of these separate, yet concurrent dramatic stories, are the "Follies" numbers, brilliantly effective, musically attractive and most elaborate.

After *The Great Ziegfeld* proved to be a great success and won the Academy Award as best picture of 1936, MGM decided that another Follies picture might do as well. William Anthony McGuire, who had written the script for the film based on the life of Florenz Ziegfeld, was assigned to write the screenplay for what was to become *Ziegfeld Girl*. Joan Crawford, Eleanor Powell, Virginia Bruce and Walter Pidgeon were lined up to play major roles. However, many problems beset the project from the start, one of which was the sudden death of McGuire, and the production was halted.

The filming of *Ziegfeld Girl* finally got under way again in October 1940 and was released in April of the following year. A completely new cast was assembled with Judy Garland, Hedy Lamarr and Lana Turner as the female stars who become Follies girls. Notable in supporting roles were Eve Arden as a hard-as-nails showgirl veteran, Rose Hobart as the brave wife of Tony Martin, and Charles Winninger as the washed-up vaudevillian father of Judy Garland.

Hedy almost didn't get *Ziegfeld Girl* due to her previous conflict with the studio. Louis B. Mayer was still angry over the troubles she caused him when she announced that she would go to New York and appear on the Broadway stage as *Salome*. As a threat to frighten his rebel star, he signed Baranova of the Ballet Russe de Monte Carlo on the pretense of starring her as Sandra.

Not a musical performer, Hedy ordinarily would not have been considered for a musical picture, but cast only as a showgirl, she had neither to sing nor to dance. Because of her super good looks, all she had to do during the lavish production numbers was look ravishing while parading around in Adrian's stunning costumes. This plus Ray June's photography brought even more excitement to the Busby Berkeley musical numbers. Also not to be overlooked are Hedy's few dramatic scenes, which she handled with fine sensitivity.

H. M. PULHAM, ESQ.

A Metro-Goldwyn-Mayer Picture   (1941)

CREDITS

Directed by King Vidor. *Screenplay by* King Vidor *and* Elizabeth Hill. *Based on the novel by* John P. Marquand. *Director of photography,* Ray June. *Art direction by* Cedric Gibbons *and* Malcolm Brown. *Set decoration by* Edwin B. Willis. *Gowns by* Kalloch. *Men's costumes by* Gile Steele. *Music score by* Bronislau Kaper. *Musical direction by* Lennie Hayton. *Recording director,* Douglas Shearer. *Film editor,* Harold F. Kress. *Running time, 119 minutes.*

CAST

Marvin Myles, HEDY LAMARR; *Harry Pulham,* ROBERT YOUNG; *Kay Motford,* RUTH HUSSEY; *Mr. Pulham, Sr.,* CHARLES COBURN; *Bill King,* VAN HEFLIN; *Mrs. Pulham,* FAY HOLDEN; *Mary Pulham,* BONITA GRANVILLE; *Mr. Bullard,* DOUGLAS WOOD; *Walter Kaufman,* CHARLES HALTON; *Rodney "Bo-Jo" Brown,* LEIF ERICKSON; *Joe Bingham,* PHIL BROWN; *Hugh (the butler),* DAVID CLYDE; *Miss Rollo,* SARA HADEN; *Skipper,* WALTER KINGSFORD; *Harry (as a boy),* BOBBY COOPER; *Chris Evans,* EARLE DEWEY; *Curtis Cole,* BYRON FOULGER; *Bob Ridge,* HARRY CROCKER; *Charley Roberts,* HARRY BROWN; *Sam Green,* DOUGLASS NEWLAND; *Sammy Lee,* GRANT WITHERS; *Tillie,* CONNIE GILCHRIST; *Sergeant,* FRANK FAYLEN; *Miss Redfern,* ANNE REVERE; *Soldier,* JOHN RAITT; *Mrs. Prindle,* OTTOLA NESMITH

As Marvin Myles

With Robert Young

With Phil Brown, Bonita Granville, Van Heflin, Robert Young and Ruth Hussey

SYNOPSIS

Harry Pulham, born and raised in the conventional, wealthy atmosphere of a Boston family, has been married for twenty years to Kay Motford.

Working on his biography for his class reunion, Harry looks back on his life. After returning from the war, he had decided to break away from his family and work in an advertising agency in New York. There he had met a beautiful copy writer, Marvin Myles. They had fallen in love, but the death of his father had brought him back to Boston.

Harry had pleaded with Marvin to marry him. But she had told him of her dislike for the stuffy life there and refused. She begged him to remain in New York.

Their parting had been a sad one, but Marvin had told him that she would always wait for him.

While he is working on his biography, he is surprised to receive a call from Marvin, who is visiting Boston. He promises to meet her. She is waiting for him, older, obviously successful, but still beautiful. The years seemed to have slipped away.

It is obvious that the old love is still there. However, they both realize that they cannot turn back twenty years.

There is another sad farewell for them, and Harry Pulham goes back to the quiet contentment of his wife and home.

REVIEWS

LOOK

Hedy Lamarr is the major news interest in the Metro-Goldwyn-Mayer picturization of *H.M. Pulham, Esq.* Miss Lamarr gave her best previous performance in *Comrade X,* with King Vidor as her director. She gave her best of all in *Pulham* and again she is under Vidor's guidance in her remarkably well-played portrayal of Marvin Myles, the smart American businesswoman of the period of the First World War.

MOVIE-RADIO GUIDE

Hedy Lamarr becomes a great actress in *H.M. Pulham, Esq.* . . . Hedy does take her longest step upward from the nautilus-shell of sheer feminine glamour. She loosens up more than ever before and turns in a grand performance. . . . Her role may not win her an Oscar. But it will undoubtedly go a long way toward establishing her as the outstanding actress she yearns to be.

DALLAS MORNING NEWS

Mr. Vidor's control is so absolute that several actors are amazingly good in roles for which nobody else would have cast them. . . . Hedy Lamarr, divested of glamour and presented as a down-to-earth career girl from Iowa (with a line to justify traces of the Viennese accent) gives the most admirable performance of her career.

HOLLYWOOD REPORTER

Every performance in the film achieves memorable quality. . . . Hedy Lamarr undertakes the assignment of a business girl, Marvin Myles, and pre-production critics were quick to voice their objections to her so-called miscasting. The manner in which Miss Lamarr comes through puts to a glorious end all the controversy, leaving her critics with a lot of words to eat. She does Marvin Myles, the girl Pulham might have married, so that it is impossible to imagine another actress in the part—that's how excellent she is.

She was waiting for him, older, but still beautiful

With Phil Brown, Ruth Hussey and Robert Young

With Robert Young and Fay Holden

PM REVIEWS

Hedy Lamarr as the woman in his (Pulham's) life is astonishing: she's wonderful. Freed here of the rigid mask of glamour, she's human, warm, beautiful and responsive.

RICHMOND (VA.) NEWS LEADER

Hedy is becoming an actress. Besides being breathtakingly beautiful as ever, she is realizing that an actress has to do more than look like one. As the forthright and capable businesswoman, she is surprisingly good.

NOTES

King Vidor, who had directed *Comrade X* and gotten such a splendid performance out of Hedy, did so again in *H.M. Pulham, Esq.* She was probably understood and handled better by Vidor than any other director who worked with her. As the smart career girl, she had the most challenging role of her career, and she was wonderful.

H.M. Pulham, Esq. is a long film that runs nearly two hours, but it is a film that holds the viewer throughout. Vidor and Elizabeth Hill wrote the intelligent screenplay based on the best-selling novel by John P. Marquand. Vidor seemed to have a keen feeling for the Bostonian atmosphere of the twenties, which showed in the special style and flair of his direction.

With Akim Tamiroff, Sheldon Leonard, Spencer Tracy and John Garfield

TORTILLA FLAT

A Metro-Goldwyn-Mayer Picture   (1942)

CREDITS

Directed by Victor Fleming. *Produced by* Sam Zimbalist. *Screenplay by* John Lee Mahin *and* Benjamin Glazer. *Based on the novel by* John Steinbeck. *Director of photography,* Karl Freund. *Art direction by* Cedric Gibbons *and* Paul Groesse. *Set decoration by* Edwin B. Willis. *Gowns by* Kalloch. *Men's costumes by* Gile Steele. *Makeup by* Jack Dawn. *Music by* Franz Waxman. *Lyrics by* Frank Loesser. *Special effects by* Warren Newcombe. *Film editor,* James E. Newcom. *Running time, 105 minutes.*

As Delores (Sweets) Ramirez

CAST

Pilon, SPENCER TRACY; *Dolores (Sweets) Ramirez,* HEDY LAMARR; *Danny,* JOHN GARFIELD; *The Pirate,* FRANK MORGAN; *Pablo,* AKIM TAMIROFF; *Tito Ralph,* SHELDON LEONARD; *José Maria Corcoran,* JOHN QUALEN; *Paul D. Cummings,* DONALD MEEK; *Mrs. Torrelli,* CONNIE GILCHRIST; *Portagee Joe,* ALLEN JENKINS; *Father Ramon,* HENRY O'NEILL; *Mrs. Marellis,* MERCEDES RUFFINO; *Señora Teresina,* MINA CAMPANA; *Brown,* ARTHUR SPACE; *Cesca,* BETTY WELLS; *Torrelli,* HARRY BURNS

With John Garfield

With Spencer Tracy
and John Garfield

SYNOPSIS

Two lazy *paisanos,* Pilon and Pablo, are thinking up schemes that might provide them with a free meal. They are interrupted by a lawyer looking for their friend Danny, who is temporarily in jail. Danny learns that his grandfather has left him two houses on Tortilla Flat.

He rents one house to Pilon and keeps the other for himself. As a property owner, Danny feels he now can court Dolores, a pretty cannery worker. But she refuses his attentions because of his laziness. In the meantime, he loses one of his houses in a fire.

Arriving in town is Pirate, with his dogs. Suspecting that the old man has money, Pilon invites him to live at Danny's house. Planning to steal Pirate's money, Pilon tells him the dangers of having his money buried.

To Pilon's surprise, Pirate trusts his money bag to him. But Pilon guards the money with his life when Pirate informs him that he has saved it to buy a golden candlestick for St. Francis, who had answered his prayers when one of his dogs was sick.

After a quarrel with Dolores, Danny goes on a drunken spree and is seriously injured. Dolores blames Pilon for causing the fight. Pilon goes to church and prays for Danny's recovery.

Danny gets well and is married to Dolores. A raffle is held that makes enough money to buy Danny a fishing boat, but no one is aware that Pilon earned the raffle money while Danny was ill.

After the newlyweds leave, Pilon philosophically reasons that owning houses started all of Danny's troubles. A match is carelessly tossed, and Danny's second house goes up in smoke.

REVIEWS

NEW YORK HERALD TRIBUNE

John Steinbeck's colorful account of California paisanos has been made into an eminently satisfying and entertaining film. *Tortilla Flat* is as good on screen as it was bad on stage some years ago. . . . Hedy Lamarr stops posing to do some real acting as a sultry Portuguese girl.

With Spencer Tracy, John Qualen and Akim Tamiroff

It is really only when Hedy Lamarr swivel-hips into the paisanos' midst that the movie takes on a definite character and purpose. Lamarr is truly fine—no goo-goo glamour girl this time, but a full-bosomed, clean-limbed peasant with spunk and sparkle enough to drive even a paisano to work as the price of her favor.

VARIETY

From John Steinbeck's book of related stories, *Tortilla Flat,* Metro has made a sincere, tender, beguiling and at times exalting picture. It is sympathetically and adroitly adapted, handsomely produced, expertly directed and eloquently acted. . . . Hedy Lamarr not only looks stunning as the Portuguese girl, but gives easily her best dramatic performances so far. Her posture seems self-conscious at times, but her lighter moments are well handled and she is excellent in the several emotional scenes.

SHOWMEN'S TRADE REVIEW

As a whole the picture is a masterpiece of art created from the explorings of human existence in the mud puddles of poverty, lust, and petty crime. . . . Garfield and Lamarr, as the girl in the case (this time with no glamorous wardrobe or scintillating backgrounds), give great realism to their delineation of two lovers, each suspicious of the other.

ST. LOUIS POST-DISPATCH

Readers of books have opportunity this week to contemplate what happens when a topnotch book is put into the hands of topnotch men and women of the screen. . . . No moving picture is likely to convey all the subtleties a novelist can pack into 400-odd pages. But neither is any novelist going to give you, in his cold print, all the nice things a movie has to offer. For instance, a couple hours with Hedy Lamarr right before your eyes. . . . The goodness and beauty of *Tortilla Flat* is not that of Hedy Lamarr, glamour girl, or Dolores, the good influence. But it is that of Hedy Lamarr, actress, caring for the possibly lesser things that make her Dolores a human being.

NOTES

In this fine production based on John Steinbeck's popular novel about life in a California fishing village, Hedy portrayed a hard-working cannery girl who had to contend with a bunch of lazy bums. She is a delight to watch as she puts the louts in their place and turns in one of her finest performances.

She acted with Spencer Tracy again for the third but, fortunately for her, the last time. Finding it extremely uncomfortable to work with him, the experience was made somewhat easier on this film due to the patience and astute direction of Victor Fleming.

Although not allowed to grab honors away from Tracy, John Garfield, on loan from Warner Brothers, was good as Danny. The supporting cast was also first-rate, made up of several of Hollywood's best character actors. Particularly fine were Akim Tamiroff, John Qualen, and Frank Morgan, the latter receiving an Oscar nomination for his eloquent performance.

With Allen Jenkins, Connie Gilchrist, Spencer Tracy, John Garfield, Mina Campana, John Qualen and Frank Morgan

With Basil Rathbone and William Powell

CROSSROADS
A Metro-Goldwyn-Mayer Picture   (1942)

CREDITS

Directed by Jack Conway. *Produced by* Edwin Knopf. *Screenplay by* Gus Trosper. *Original story by* John Kafka *and* Howard Emmett Rogers. *Director of photography,* Joseph Ruttenberg. *Art direction by* Cedric Gibbons *and* John S. Detlie. *Set decoration by* Edwin B. Willis. *Gowns by* Kalloch. *Music by* Bronislau Kaper. *Song, "Till You Remember," by* Arthur Schwartz *and* Howard Dietz. *Recording director,* Douglas Shearer. *Film editor,* George Boemler. *Running time, 82 minutes.*

As Lucienne Talbot

CAST

David Talbot, WILLIAM POWELL; *Lucienne Talbot,* HEDY LAMARR; *Michele Allaine,* CLAIRE TREVOR; *Henri Sarrou,* BASIL RATHBONE; *Mme. Pelletier,* MARGARET WYCHERLY; *Dr. Andre Tessier,* FELIX BRESSART; *Dr. Alex Dubroc,* SIG RUMANN; *Prosecuting Attorney,* H. B. WARNER; *Commissaire,* PHILIP MERIVALE; *Carlos Le Duc,* VLADIMIR SOKOLOFF; *President of Court,* GUY BATES POST; *Duval,* FRITZ LEIBER; *Baron De Lorrain,* JOHN MYLONG; *Defense Attorney,* FRANK CONROY; *Martin,* JAMES RENNIE; *Pierre,* BERTRAM MARBROUGH; *Asst. Defense Attorney,* HARRY FLEISCHMAN

With William Powell

With Claire Trevor

SYNOPSIS

Lucienne and David Talbot have recently married. David, a diplomat in the French Foreign Office, receives an ominous note demanding that he repay a million-franc debt, of which he knows nothing.

Carlos Le Duc, the extortionist, is brought to trial; he bases his defense on the claim that the debt is a just one and that David is really Jean Pelletier, a criminal who had borrowed money from him and then disappeared. David had been injured years ago and remembers nothing of his previous life.

Through Michele Allaine, the defense substantiates its claim that he is Pelletier. She intimates that David had been her lover. But the surprise testimony of Henri Sarrou stops the trial when he testifies that he had been with Pelletier the night he died.

Le Duc is pronounced guilty, and David is cleared. Sarrou visits David and reveals that his testimony had been false. He declares that David is actually Pelletier and that he, Sarrou, had been his accomplice.

He further reveals that he is the blackmailer and that the million francs demanded is due him from a robbery-murder the two had committed.

David begins to believe the story when he is shown a photograph of himself in an intimate pose with Michele. Lucienne, sensing David's danger, asks Dr. Tessier to speak with him.

David learns from the doctor that the injury he had suffered was on the right side of the head, the side on which he used to part his hair. Because of the stitches, he now parts his hair on the left side. The picture with Michele shows that his hair was parted on the left side. David realizes that it is a recent photo of him and a fake. With police aid, he cleverly traps Sarrou.

With Basil Rathbone

REVIEWS

NEW YORK POST

If *Crossroads* finds favor with the movie-going public, it will be because it is a good production, well cast down to the minor parts and directed intelligently. Regarded simply on its own merits, it deserves a measure of praise. . . . Miss Lamarr is entirely adequate as an actress and more than adequate as something to dream about.

NEW YORK HERALD TRIBUNE

It is not often that the screen goes in for psychological melodrama. When it is handled as adroitly as it is in the new picture, the entertainment quotient is considerable. *Crossroads* has a tricky script, expert direction, and the invaluable collaboration of William Powell. . . . He succeeds in inspiring Hedy Lamarr, as he has inspired so many of his leading women, to do a real job of acting here. For Miss Lamarr is always solidly supporting the subjective implications of the continuity. Whether she is steadfastly behind her celebrated husband in a courtroom scene, or torn by doubts after the blackmailers have worked their supposedly perfect job, she is far more persuasive than I have ever seen her.

With Claire Trevor,
William Powell
and Basil Rathbone

With William Powell

With Basil Rathbone and William Powell

NOTES

VARIETY

This is a grade A whodunit, with a superlative cast . . . Miss Lamarr delivers here one of her best acting jobs to date; for once it's not merely a matter of being beautiful.

NEW YORK DAILY MIRROR

There's some fine acting all the way; but Lamarr is the big special. She's superb—and looks it.

GREATER AMUSEMENTS

Splendid acting, excellent direction and skillful production technique have been closely aligned in making of this interesting and very human picture. . . . Performances of the stars are superb especially that of Hedy Lamarr, whose beauty and glamor have been supplemented by a polished portrayal.

MGM went all out with this mystery, which had a working title of *The Man Who Lost His Way* but was released as *Crossroads*. No expense was spared in gowning the ladies or on the elaborate sets constructed for the picture, but the result was a lumbering, confusing film.

Hedy was lovely to watch as the sophisticated bride. But she wasn't given much to do, which was quite vexing since she had a great deal of footage in the film. William Powell's work as the confused diplomat wasn't up to his standard brand of acting, which he had displayed so wonderfully in his Thin Man movies. The role should have been played by Charles Boyer.

Claire Trevor's part was so ill conceived that she was unable to pull it off with any kind of believability. Hedy, however, regarded her as a good actress and liked working with her. The Trevor role had originally been offered to Marlene Dietrich, who nixed the part by bluntly stating, "I'll share glamour with nobody!"

At this time, MGM announced plans for two more films for Hedy that never came to fruition. In the first, she would have been a Russian guerrilla in *Scorched Earth*. The second would have reteamed her with Robert Taylor in something to be called *The Last Time I Saw Paris*. Metro used that title several years later as an Elizabeth Taylor starrer.

Preceding page: With Walter Pidgeon

CREDITS

Directed by Richard Thorpe. *Produced by* Victor Saville. *Screenplay by* Leon Gordon *from his stage play. Based on the novel Hell's Playground by* Ida Vera Simonton. *Director of photography,* Harry Stradling. *Art direction by* Cedric Gibbons *and* Daniel B. Cathcart. *Set decoration by* Edwin B. Willis. *Costumes by* Kalloch. *Makeup created by* Jack Dawn. *Music by* Bronislau Kaper. *Dance direction by* Ernest Matray. *Recording director,* Douglas Shearer. *Film editor,* Frederick Y. Smith. *Running time, 90 minutes.*

CAST

Tondelayo, HEDY LAMARR; *Harry Witzel,* WALTER PIDGEON; *The Doctor,* FRANK MORGAN; *Langford,* RICHARD CARLSON; *Skipper,* REGINALD OWEN; *Reverend Roberts,* HENRY O'NEILL; *Wilbur Ashley,* BRAMWELL FLETCHER; *Ted,* CLYDE COOK; *Jim Flash,* LEIGH WHIPPER; *Umeela,* OSCAR POLK; *Doctor's Houseboy,* DARBY JONES; *Worthing,* RICHARD AINLEY

SYNOPSIS

Deep in Africa, Harry Witzel, a cynical but determined man, oversees a rubber station. He has become disgusted with his assistant, Wilbur Ashley, who has deteriorated in both mind and body.

Ashley, no longer of use to himself or anyone else, is forced to leave his job and return home. He is replaced by handsome young Langford.

Langford is determined to maintain his propriety and not let the conditions of Africa get the better of him. He is warned by Witzel to watch out for a beautiful native girl, Tondelayo, known by all to be a temptress.

Before long, Tondelayo learns of Langford's presence and visits him at his bungalow. She is soon discovered by Witzel and sent away. Langford can get no work out of the natives; they continually disobey his orders. Gradually, his deterioration starts.

Tondelayo returns, and Langford is wild to see her. He wants to marry her. Witzel tries to discourage him, but he will not listen. It is disclosed that Tondelayo is a white woman, the daughter of an Egyptian; therefore, they are free to marry.

As Tondelayo

With Richard Carlson

With Frank Morgan and Henry O'Neill

With Leigh Whipper

When Langford is stricken with fever, Tondelayo is discovered poisoning him. Disenchanted with her marriage, she has decided to get rid of him. Witzel sees what she is doing and forces her to drink the poison. Clutching her throat, she runs into the jungle and dies.

Langford recovers and is sent home. Witzel once again has to break in a new man. But this time there is no Tondelayo around to bewitch him.

With Richard Carlson

Tondelayo dances

168

REVIEWS

VARIETY

Miss Lamarr is the only femme in the film and is doing her best acting to date, although the part is a natural for any girl with a halfway good physical appearance. The brunette beauty doesn't have to take a backseat to any sarong-wearer. Plus this, she delivers a cooch dance that's more Minsky than Afriko. Lamarr dancing has as much exploitation value as Garbo laughing—perhaps more, considering how the former dances.

THE INDEPENDENT

Comparisons are odious, but Hedy Lamarr in a sarong and Mother Hubbard loincloth is incomparable. Hedy will be the reason for the success of *White Cargo*, the entire picture about the uncanny disintegration of a white man in the tropics being obviously nothing more than a pretext to allow Hedy to show her considerable and well-distributed charms. . . . There are some good actors, whom it is pleasant to see again . . . But, for the American public, there will be only one magnet in *White Cargo*—Hedy Lamarr.

THE HARTFORD TIMES

An entertaining story with good portrayals. . . . Shown as a copper-skinned siren, there is a great deal of the Lamarr personality visible, more so than in some of her pictures. The Tondelayo role is somewhat better than that in *Ecstasy*, we think.

BOXOFFICE

The general treatment and atmosphere of Leon Gordon's time-honored successful stage play are the unencumbered heritage of this film version, for which he wrote the screenplay. . . . Hedy Lamarr here, body stained a rich walnut, is a natural for the Tondelayo—seductive, sexy, scorching. Her performance will bring many a whistle from the boys in the gallery. . . . Hedy Lamarr was never more exotic or ravishing. You will be thrilled by the masterful performances of a great cast.

NOTES

Leon Gordon transposed his successful 1920s play of the corruptive rot of African river landing living to the screen especially for Miss Lamarr. Hedy, as the hot-fudge-sundae temptress, gave an exciting performance of many facets: sensuous, provocative, mercenary, brazen, mesmeric.

Walter Pidgeon, as the vitriolic Witzel, likewise was good in his role. Clark Gable and Spencer Tracy had played the role in earlier stage productions. Also, another Metro player, Fay Holden (Ma Hardy), previously known as Gaby Fey, can be counted among the many actresses who had played Tondelayo on the stage.

The booze-guzzling expatriate doctor, doomed to live out his life in the tropics while trying to hang on to his threadbare dignity, was skillfully played with sympathetic compassion by Frank Morgan.

An early version of *White Cargo* was filmed in England in 1929 with Gypsy Rhouma as the serpentine Tondelayo. Maurice Evans portrayed Langford, Leslie Faber was seen as Weston (the Witzel character), and John Hamilton was Ashley.

With William Powell

THE HEAVENLY BODY
A Metro-Goldwyn-Mayer Picture (1943)

CREDITS

Directed by Alexander Hall. *Produced by* Arthur Hornblow, Jr. *Screenplay by* Michael Arlen *and* Walter Reisch. *Adaptation by* Harry Kurnitz. *Based on a story by* Jacques Thery. *Director of photography,* Robert Planck. *Art direction by* Cedric Gibbons *and* William Ferrari. *Set decoration by* Edwin B. Willis *and* McLean Nesbit. *Costumes by* Irene. *Music by* Bronislau Kaper. *Special effects by* Arnold Gillespie. *Recording director,* Douglas Shearer. *Film editor,* Blanche Sewell. *Running time,* 95 minutes.

CAST

William S. Whitley, WILLIAM POWELL; *Vicky Whitley,* HEDY LAMARR; *Lloyd Hunter,* JAMES CRAIG; *Margaret Sibyll,* FAY BAINTER; *Professor Stowe,* HENRY O'NEILL; *Nancy Potter,* SPRING BYINGTON; *Strand,* ROBERT SULLY; *Dr. Green,* MORRIS ANKRUM; *Sebastian Melas,* FRANCO CORSARO; *Beulah Murphy,* CONNIE GILCHRIST; *Dr. Gurtchakoff,* MAX WILLENZ; *Forbes,* EARL SCHENCK; *Pierson,* ARTHUR SPACE; *Stella,* HELEN FREEMAN; *Ethel,* PHYLLIS KENNEDY; *Pearl Harrison,* MARIETTA CANTY; *Willie,* NICODEMUS; *Nicholas,* HOWARD MITCHELL; *Frank,* DAN B. SHEFFIELD; *Mrs. Potter's Mother,* GERTRUDE W. HOFFMAN; *Vladimir,* ALEX MELESH; *Porter,* JAMES BASQUETTE

As Vicky Whitley   With James Craig

With Spring Byington

With Helen Freeman and Fay Bainter

On the set with her stand-in Sylvia Hollis

SYNOPSIS

Feeling neglected because Bill, her astronomer-husband, is preoccupied with a new comet, Vicky Whitley seeks some diversion. She meets an astrologer who tells her that, by the twenty-second of the month, she will fall in love with a man who has traveled widely.

Vicky informs Bill of the prediction. Upset at her belief in astrology, Bill leaves her and goes to his observatory. Vicky patiently waits for her "man" to appear. After an uneventful day on the twenty-second, she telephones Bill; admitting that she was wrong, she asks him to return home.

Just as midnight approaches, Lloyd Hunter, an air raid warden, reprimands Vicky for violating a blackout rule. She questions him and learns that he has traveled extensively. Bill arrives home just as Lloyd leaves and senses Vicky's reaction.

The next day, Bill asks Lloyd to change his district. But Lloyd has fallen in love with Vicky. Despite Bill's effort to keep them apart, fate keeps throwing Vicky and Lloyd together.

Hoping that it will save his marriage, Bill visits the astrologer and compels her to write a fake horoscope for Vicky, foretelling his death. He feigns illness to gain her sympathy, but Vicky learns of the fake horoscope.

Bill gives up hope and leaves again. Lloyd urges Vicky to go to Reno for a divorce, but she changes her mind at the last minute and reconciles with Bill.

REVIEWS

HOLLYWOOD REPORTER

The Heavenly Body is strictly escapist stuff, designed for laugh purposes only. . . . Powell is completely at home in the type of role he plays here and gives it the polished performance to be expected, which means it could not be done better. To her loveliness, excellently photographed, Hedy Lamarr adds a consistently improving acting ability, her performance in this reflecting her work with the capable Jean Hathaway.

With James Craig

FILM DAILY

A titillating marital farce, *The Heavenly Body* is first-rate fun that will draw handsomely, thanks no little to the pairing of William Powell and Hedy Lamarr in the top roles. The film tells a diverting story smartly and with considerable bounce. . . . Powell is the main show in *The Heavenly Body*. Miss Lamarr is chiefly ornamental. James Craig, Miss Bainter, Henry O'Neill, Spring Byington deliver the best performances in the supporting roles.

BROOKLYN CITIZEN

Miss Lamarr was never more beautiful than as she appears in a special wardrobe by Irene. In her first attempt at light comedy she carries off her role with the assurance of a veteran.

PM REVIEWS

As bores go, *The Heavenly Body* is something rather special, in that it offers the ultra-luxury of being bored by no less a personage than Hedy Lamarr.

With William Powell and Connie Gilchrist

NOTES

Many talents were wasted by MGM when they were used in this unimportant farce, which doesn't have any more value than a half hour of television situation comedy.

Powell and Fay Bainter certainly deserved better material than this inferior property, which Hedy wound up with when she unwisely turned down *Dragon Seed*.

The script, containing silly situations and stupid dialogue, was so poorly written that even a talented director like Alexander Hall couldn't do anything with it. However, wartime audiences were not too fussy about what they saw. They would watch any film that would help keep their minds off the horrors going on in Europe and the Pacific. So *The Heavenly Body* earned some money for Metro while the Lamarr name blazed on theater marquees.

With Victor Francen, Peter Lorre, Louis Mercier, Gregory Gay and Sydney Greenstreet

THE CONSPIRATORS

A Warner Bros. Picture   (1944)

CREDITS

With Peter Lorre and Victor Francen

Directed by Jean Negulesco. *Produced by* Jack Chertok. *Screenplay by* Vladimir Pozner *and* Leo Rosten. *Additional dialogue by* Jack Moffitt. *Based on a novel by* Fredric Prokosch. *Director of photography,* Arthur Edeson. *Art direction by* Anton Grot. *Set decoration by* Walter Tilford. *Gowns by* Leah Rhodes. *Music by* Max Steiner. *Musical director,* Leo F. Forbstein. *Orchestral arrangements by* Leonid Raab. *Special effects by* Willard Van Enger, William McGann, *and* James Leicester. *Film editor,* Rudi Fehr. *Running time, 101 minutes.*

CAST

Irene, HEDY LAMARR; *Vincent Van der Lyn,* PAUL HENREID; *Quintanilla,* SYDNEY GREENSTREET; *Bernazsky,* PETER LORRE; *Hugo von Mohr,* VICTOR FRANCEN; *Capt. Pereira,* JOSEPH CALLEIA; *Rosa,* CAROL THURSTON; *Miguel,* VLADIMIR SOKO-LOFF; *Almeida,* EDUARDO CIANNELLI; *Dr. Schmidt,* STEVEN GERAY; *Lutzke,* KURT KATCH; *Wynat,* GREGORY GAY; *Croupier,* MARCEL DALIO; *The Con Man,* GEORGE MACREADY; *Mrs. Benson,* DORIS LLOYD; *Leiris,* LOUIS MERCIER; *Jennings,* MONTE BLUE; *Page Boy,* BILLY ROY; *Antonio,* DAVID HOFFMAN; *The Slugger,* OTTO REICHOW; *Waiter,* LEON BELASCO; *Casino Attendant,* FRANK REISCHNER

As Irene von Mohr

175

With Paul Henried

SYNOPSIS

In 1944, refugees of Nazi-occupied Europe flee to Lisbon, the takeoff point to America and safety. And to the city come soldiers of fortune, Nazi and anti-Nazi. Arriving in Lisbon to contact a group of confederates, Vincent Van der Lyn, a Dutch underground agent, is directed to a cafe where he receives instructions from Bernazsky, a fellow conspirator.

At the cafe, Vincent meets Irene, who rushes in and seats herself at his table to escape the police.

When she disappears from the cafe, he follows her to Estoril, a gambling casino. She pleads with him to forget her. The next day, Vincent meets Quintanilla, head of the conspirators, who instructs him to give information to another agent that night.

In the meantime, Vincent induces Irene to spend the day with him. Both fall in love despite the fact that she is married to Hugo von Mohr, a member of the German legation.

Vincent returns to his hotel room to meet the agent, only to find the man murdered. The police arrive and arrest him for the killing. Believing that he is the victim of a Nazi plot engineered by Irene, Vincent escapes from jail and joins Quintanilla. He learns that both Irene and her husband are members of their group.

Quintanilla announces that the murder may have been committed by a traitor among their own group. He and Vincent set a trap to catch the traitor.

Von Mohr reveals himself as the guilty person and is shot trying to escape. In his pocket, the police find evidence clearing Vincent of the murder.

Vincent leaves on another mission, promising Irene that he will soon return to her.

REVIEWS

FILM DAILY

An intriguing spy meller, splendidly cast, richly produced, definitely pulsating entertainment. Jack Chertok has spared little in giving Hedy Lamarr a worthwhile production for her first Warner effort. On the other hand, Hedy does well by the producer in breathing glamour into a spy role that adds lustre to the entire offering. . . . Jean Negulesco's direction of a script that gives an array of attractive feature names equal opportunity to share acting honors, is interesting, suspenseful, and arresting. There is much that has been injected to give more to a general audience than they may expect.

With Victor Francen

With Paul Henried

With Eduardo Ciannelli and Victor Francen

You can't trust anybody in *The Conspirators,* not even Hedy Lamarr—and such a pretty thing, too. The picture, which employs practically the entire Warner stock company, is in the spirit of high adventure which characterized *Mask of Dimitrios,* also directed by Jean Negulesco. And like most exotic melodrama in the tradition of *Casablanca,* it makes a good show.

The best thing about *The Conspirators* is its cast—Hedy Lamarr, Paul Henreid, Sydney Greenstreet and Peter Lorre, whose talents deserve a lot better showcase than the current Warner attraction.

Both Mr. Henreid and Miss Lamarr in the two leading roles give good accounts of themselves, as do Messrs. Greenstreet and Lorre and Victor Francen.

NOTES

MGM loaned Hedy to Warner Bros. to head the cast of *The Conspirators,* a film adapted from Fredric Prokosch's novel dealing with wartime intrigue in Lisbon.

Patterned along the same lines as *Casablanca,* with the hope of equal success, Warners spent a good part of their budget for the elaborate sets constructed for the film. Anton Grot outdid himself with his splendid creations of the Estoril gambling casino (the Monte Carlo of Portugal), the Cafe Imperium, Lisbon streets, sumptuous boudoirs, and quaint antique shops. Academy members were blinded to the fact that they were the year's best sets and failed to bestow even one nomination. The gowns Leah Rhodes designed for Miss Lamarr were lovely and elegant and in keeping with what the wife of a high-ranking official would wear. Max Steiner, one of filmdom's most talented composers (*Gone with the Wind; Now, Voyager; Johnny Belinda*), contributed another of his excellent scores, which set the mood for suspense and romance.

The supporting cast is a good one, with several members of the *Casablanca* cast on hand. Outstanding in interesting roles are Sydney Greenstreet and Victor Francen. As scene after scene reveals one familiar Teutonic face after the other, one seems to be continually waiting for a glimpse of Helmut Dantine, Conrad Veidt, or S. Z. Sakall, all of whom somehow got left out of the proceedings.

With George Brent

EXPERIMENT PERILOUS
An R.K.O. Radio Picture   (1944)

CREDITS

Directed by Jacques Tourneur. *Produced by* Robert Fellows. *Screenplay by* Warren Duff. *Based on a novel by* Margaret Carpenter. *Director of photography,* Tony Gaudio. *Art direction by* Albert S. D'Agostino *and* Jack Okey. *Set decoration by* Darrell Silvera *and* Claude Carpenter. *Gowns for Miss Lamarr by* Leah Rhodes. *Other gowns by* Edward Stevenson. *Music by* Roy Webb. *Musical director,* C. Bakaleinikoff. *Special effects by* Vernon L. Walker. *Film editor,* Ralph Dawson. *Running time, 92 minutes.*

CAST

Allida, HEDY LAMARR; *Dr. Hunt Bailey,* GEORGE BRENT; *Nick Bederaux,* PAUL LUKAS; *Claghorne,* ALBERT DEKKER; *Maitland,* CARL ESMOND; *Cissie Bederaux,* OLIVE BLAKENEY; *Alec,* GEORGE N. NEISE; *Maggie,* MARGARET WYCHERLY; *Elaine,* STEPHANIE BACHELOR; *Miss Wilson,* MARY SERVOSS; *Deria,* JULIA DEAN; *Alec Bederaux,* BILLY WARD; *District Attorney,* WILLIAM POST, JR.; *Bellhop,* NOLAN LEARY; *Caterer,* LARRY WHEAT; *Porter,* SAM McDANIELS; *Train Steward,* EDWARD CLARK; *Frank,* BRODERICK O'FARRELL; *Salesgirl,* LILLIAN WEST; *Clerk,* ALMEDA FOWLER; *Voice Instructors,* GEORGES RENAVENT, ADRIENNE D'AMBRICOURT; *Ballet Master,* MICHAEL VISAROFF; *Nick, Sr.,* JOHN MYLONG; *Nick (at age 3),* MICHAEL ORR; *Cissie (at age 8),* PEGGY MILLER

With Paul Lukas

As Allida Bederaux

With Carl Esmond, George Brent and Albert Dekker

With Paul Lukas

With George Brent

SYNOPSIS

On a train bound for New York, Dr. Hunt Bailey becomes acquainted with Cissie Bederaux, a talkative spinster. She tells him that she is on her way to a birthday party for her sister-in-law Allida. Allida is married to Cissie's brother, Nick, a famed philanthropist.

Later that night at a party, Hunt overhears that Cissie has died of a heart attack soon after reaching the Bederaux home. Suspicious, Hunt arranges through Claghorne, a friend, to visit the Bederaux home for tea.

There, Hunt finds himself caught by Allida's striking beauty and also becomes aware that she is in great fear of something.

He becomes disturbed when Bederaux takes him aside and insinuates that Allida is mentally unsound. The next day, Bederaux visits Hunt to discuss Allida's mental state.

Hunt finds Bederaux's statements contrary to many things Cissie had told him. He becomes convinced that Allida is afraid of Bederaux because of an indiscretion she apparently had committed with a young poet, who later was found dead.

Having fallen in love with Allida and fearing for her life, Hunt arranges to move her and her small son to a place of safety. Bederaux learning of the plan, traps Hunt in the Bederaux home and informs him that the house is filled with gas and soon will explode.

Meanwhile, he confesses to the murders of the poet and Cissie, who had known he was insane. Hunt attacks the deranged man and manages to save Allida and her son before the explosion, which kills Bederaux.

REVIEWS

HOLLYWOOD REPORTER

Nothing short of inspired casting brings Hedy Lamarr to play the role of a woman of such haunting beauty that every man who sees her falls in love with her. From the circumstances surrounding the actions of an insanely jealous husband, Margaret Carpenter wove an extraordinary novel of psychological mystery which immediately won critical acclaim and lifted *Experiment Perilous* to the ranks of a best-seller last season. As a motion picture of fascinating mood and suspense, it has found an adroit realization through the superlative work of its central players and its admirable presentation. . . . Miss Lamarr might have been content merely to provide visual charms to her role of the lovely Mrs. Bederaux. Her advancement as an actress, however, matches her beauty and she gives a splendid performance. It is the most mature portrayal of her career.

With George Brent, Paul Lukas, Albert Dekker and Carl Esmond

VARIETY

Hedy Lamarr contributes a surprise performance with adroit shadings of terror, romantic interest, eerie characterization, and manages to separate the wife's young maidenhood and the distraught mother's fear about her son with genuine span of maturity.

NEW YORK MORNING TELEGRAPH

Experiment Perilous holds attention from the opening shot and builds dramatically up to the sensational fadeout. Miss Lamarr brings dramatic brilliance to her role and George Brent strikes just the right note as Hunt.

NOTES

Hedy got one of the best roles of her career when Metro agreed to loan her to RKO for *Experiment Perilous.* It was one of several psychological mysteries that studio was known for that later included Dorothy McGuire's haunting *The Spiral Staircase.*

Hedy's performance was a lovely portrait of a woman worshiped by everyone who met her. A woman of elegant loveliness, she was also one who was in mortal danger from an insane husband who was intent on killing her.

The production values of the film were of the highest quality. Tony Gaudio's beautiful photography complemented Hedy's serene beauty as well as capturing the menacing mood of a magnificent old New York mansion. The sets were brilliantly designed by Albert S. D'Agostino, Jack Okey, Darrell Silvera, and Claude Carpenter, all of whom received Academy Award nominations for their fine work. Miss Lamarr's fabulous wardrobe of turn-of-the-century gowns was designed by Leah Rhodes, who had done the clothes for *The Conspirators.*

With June Allyson and Robert Walker

HER HIGHNESS AND THE BELLBOY

A Metro-Goldwyn-Mayer Picture   (1945)

With Warner Anderson

CREDITS

Directed by Richard Thorpe. *Produced by* Joe Pasternak. *Screenplay by* Richard Connell *and* Gladys Lehman. *Director of photography,* Harry Stradling. *Art Direction by* Cedric Gibbons *and* Urie McCleary. *Set decoration by* Edwin B. Willis. *Costumes by* Marion Herwood Keyes *and* Valles. *Music by* Georgie Stoll. *Orchestrations by* Calvin Jackson. *Dance direction by* Charles Walters. *Film editor,* George Boemler. *Running time, 108 minutes.*

CAST

Princess Veronica, HEDY LAMARR; *Jimmy Dobson,* ROBERT WALKER; *Leslie Odell,* JUNE ALLYSON; *Baron Zoltan Faludi,* CARL ESMOND; *Countess Zoe,* AGNES MOOREHEAD; *Albert Weever,* "RAGS" RAGLAND; *Mr. Pufi,* LUDWIG STOSSEL; *Dr. Elfson,* GEORGE CLEVELAND; *Paul MacMillan,* WARNER ANDERSON; *Yanos von Lankofitz,* KONSTANTIN SHAYNE; *Hack,* TOM TROUT; *Himself,* BEN LESSY; *Fae,* PATTY MOORE; *First Policeman,* EDWARD GARGAN; *Countess Tradiska,* ANN CODEE; *Mr. Fabler,* FERDINAND MUNIER; *Mr. Korb,* EMIL RAMEAU; *Pearl,* GLADYS BLAKE; *Mrs. Korb,* OLGA FABIAN; *Mr. Pook,* JACK NORTON; *Mildred,* AUDREY TOTTER; *Mrs. Chudduster,* GRAYCE HAMPTON; *Police Captain Perie,* WILLIAM HALLIGAN; *Aunt Gertrude Odell,* VIRGINIA SALE; *Woman,* BESS FLOWERS; *Diplomat's Wife,* BETTY BLYTHE

With Robert Walker

As Princess Veronica

With Warner Anderson, Robert Walker, June Allyson and "Rags" Ragland

SYNOPSIS

Princess Veronica visits New York, hoping to see Paul MacMillan, a reporter with whom she had fallen in love when he visited her country. At her hotel, Jimmy Dobson, a bellboy, mistakes her for a maid, but Veronica, amused, asks that he be assigned as her personal attendant.

Veronica arranges a meeting with MacMillan; realizing that her royal status would mar their happiness, he says that his love has cooled. Meanwhile Jimmy, misunderstanding Veronica's kindness, concludes that she loves him. This upsets Leslie Odell, a pretty young invalid who loves him and looks forward to his daily visits.

Veronica asks Jimmy to take her to a bar where MacMillan does most of his work. There they become involved in a raid; Veronica is jailed. Bailed out by MacMillan, she learns that the king is dead and that she is queen now.

She prepares to leave for Europe and informs Jimmy that he may come with her. Mistaking this for a marriage proposal, Jimmy is elated. When he goes to say good-bye to Leslie, however, he realizes that he loves her.

He informs Veronica that she must give him up. Veronica realizes that Jimmy, in order to enjoy real happiness, has rejected what he thought was his chance to be a king. Following his example, she abdicates to marry MacMillan.

REVIEWS

NATIONAL BOARD OF REVIEW MAGAZINE

Although told with painful whimsy and sentimentality, the long story has good comedy bits and several high moments, notably a dream sequence in which June dances and a fine fight when Princess Hedy goes slumming. Both stars are charming throughout the well-produced film, and the cast generally does its best with the uncertain material.

VARIETY

What contributes immensely to the enjoyment of the picture are the performances, notably of Hedy Lamarr, Robert Walker and "Rags" Ragland. . . . Miss Allyson comes close to stealing the picture in a difficult role.

HOLLYWOOD REPORTER

June Allyson, bless her, is a lovely, sincerely good little actress. . . . Hedy Lamarr comes out a real winner. Now why didn't anyone ever think of having her play gentle comedy before? Goes well with her dewy-eyed beauty.

With Ferdinand Munier, Ludwig Stossel, Marie Melish and Agnes Moorehead

PHOTOPLAY

Walker crowns himself with glory as the bellhop assigned to her Royal Highness Hedy Lamarr in a famous New York hostelry. The lad grows in stature, in charm, in authority, with every film. June Allyson as the little cripple whom he really loves has a pixie-like charm that comes across in this film with appealing cuteness. And Hedy for the first time since *Algiers* seems a woman of reality, of emotional integrity and inner beauty.

LOS ANGELES TIMES

Walker catches the public fancy and conveys comedy most aptly, while Miss Lamarr has a chance to look beautiful and act with sympathy. Miss Allyson is gently persuasive.

LOS ANGELES EXAMINER

As the heavenly-faced princess, Hedy Lamarr contributes her best performance in a long time.

NOTES

Her Highness and the Bellboy is the film Hedy elected to do instead of *Diamond Rock,* a story of a married woman's tragic love for a younger man. Perhaps *Diamond Rock* might have been a better choice, for there is hardly anything worthwhile to say about *Her Highness and the Bellboy* except that June Allyson added charm to the proceedings. The script was silly and gave director Richard Thorpe little to work with. Hedy seemed bewildered by the whole thing, and Agnes Moorehead, a fine actress, should not have been wasted in such a worthless piece of trivia.

The gowns were unimpressive, not even pretty and certainly not expensive looking enough for a princess (unless she were from England!). The sets devised were not good, either. In fact, some were leftovers from a previous Metro production, *Weekend at the Waldorf.*

With June Allyson

With Edward Gargan, Gladys Blake and William Halligan

With Gene Lockhart and Louis Hayward

THE STRANGE WOMAN

A Hunt Stromberg Production Released by United Artists   (1946)

CREDITS

Directed by Edgar Ulmer. *Produced by* Jack Chertok. *Screenplay by* Herb Meadows. *Based on the novel by* Ben Ames Williams. *Director of photography,* Lucien Andriot. *Art direction by* Nicolai Remisoff. *Costumes by* Natalie Visart. *Hair styles by* Blanche Smith. *Makeup by* Joseph Stinton. *Music by* Carmen Dragon. *Film editor,* James E. Newcom. *Running time, 100 minutes.*

CAST

Jenny Hager, HEDY LAMARR; *John Evered,* GEORGE SANDERS; *Ephraim Poster,* LOUIS HAYWARD; *Isaiah Poster,* GENE LOCKHART; *Meg Saladine,* HILLARY BROOKE; *Deacon Adams,* RHYS WILLIAMS; *Lena Tempest,* JUNE STOREY; *Reverend Thatcher,* MORONI OLSEN; *Mrs. Hollis,* OLIVE BLAKENEY; *Tim Hager,* DENNIS HOEY; *Judge Saladine,* ALAN NAPIER; *Lincoln Pittridge,* IAN KEITH; *Mr. Partridge,* EDWARD BIBY; *Miss Partridge,* KATHERINE YORK.

As Jenny Hager

SYNOPSIS

It is 1820, and beautiful Jenny Hager has reached womanhood in the rough lumber town of Bangor, Maine. Inherently cruel, she rebels against her drunken father and runs to the protection of Isaiah Poster, an aged, wealthy shopkeeper who covets her. Poster tricks several leading citizens into suggesting that he marry Jenny to protect her. Jenny agrees.

Cleverly covering up her cruel nature with a display of charity and kindness, Jenny becomes the central figure in Bangor. She induces Poster's son Ephraim to return from college. In her evil way, she taunts him into loving and desiring her.

Meanwhile, Jenny finds herself attracted to John Evered, boss of Poster's lumber camp and fiance of Meg Saladine, her best friend.

To clear the way for her conquest of Evered, Jenny promises herself to Ephraim if he will kill his father. Ephraim achieves the old man's death through a drowning accident, but Jenny, now mistress of a fortune, throws him out.

She then sets out to win Evered and eventually succeeds in marrying him. Meanwhile, Ephraim degenerates into a drunkard and kills himself.

Evered soon begins to notice Jenny's sadistic tendencies. During a quarrel, he learns her true nature when she incautiously reveals that she had prompted Ephraim to kill his father. Evered leaves her, and Meg, learning of this, goes to the lumber camp to console him.

Seeing them together, Jenny becomes enraged with jealousy and deliberately tries to run them down with her horses. But the wheels of her carriage hit a rock, and Jenny, thrown from the rig, dies.

REVIEWS

HOLLYWOOD REPORTER

Miss Lamarr, long celebrated for the exceptional beauty she presents to the camera, seemed determined to settle the question of her acting abilities once and for all. There are those who have doubted that she is an actress, others who don't care if she is or not, just so long as her image appears in the movies for everyone to admire. Now Hedy establishes her status in positive terms. In this feature, she gives a performance that can rank with the best of them. Don't be surprised to see her win an Academy nomination for her work here. . . . Obviously Miss Lamarr had to etch Jenny in the acid her lack of character demanded. Had she or Ulmer erred in softening the role, all of its grim fascination would have been lost. The star is the bewitching beauty she has always been, but she is now the acting beauty.

With Louis Hayward
and Gene Lockhart

With George Sanders

With Hillary Brooke

With Louis Hayward

SILVER SCREEN

Hedy Lamarr is cast as the troublemaker and director Edgar Ulmer, a fellow Viennese, has succeeded, where others have failed, in thawing out the actress frozen beneath the exquisite Lamarr exterior. Miss Lamarr indeed does her first acting in this opus. . . . The film manages to achieve many dramatic highs, thanks, principally, to the new Hedy.

SHOWMEN'S TRADE REVIEW

In a role quite foreign to anything she's done to date, Miss Lamarr turns in her best performance.

NOTES

The first choice for Hedy's independent company, *The Strange Woman*, was a good one, which gave her the opportunity to run the gamut of emotions. She was exceptionally good as she went from the frightened naive girl to the assured young wife of the town merchant and then the conniving woman who would stop at nothing to satisfy her selfish desires.

Edgar Ulmer, whose work is highly praised by the French film critics, directed Hedy with a sure hand, obtaining an exciting, fiery performance. Born in Vienna, he had been an actor and set designer who had worked for Max Reinhardt and, later on, made films for Decla in Berlin. He had also collaborated with Alexander Korda and F. W. Murnau before coming to the United States. Among his acclaimed works is the horror film *Bluebeard* with John Carradine.

With John Loder

DISHONORED LADY

A Hunt Stromberg Production Released by United Artists   (1947)

CREDITS

Directed by Robert Stevenson. *Produced by* Jack Chertok. *Screenplay by* Edmund H. North. *Based on a play by* Edward Sheldon *and* Margaret Ayer Barnes. *Director of photography,* Lucien Andriot. *Production design and art direction by* Nicolai Remisoff. *Gowns by* Elois Jenssen. *Music by* Carmen Dragon. *Film editor,* John Foley. *Running time, 86 minutes.*

CAST

Madeleine Damien, HEDY LAMARR; *Dr. David Cousins,* DENNIS O'KEEFE; *Felix Courtland,* JOHN LODER; *Jack Garet,* WILLIAM LUNDIGAN; *Dr. Caleb,* MORRIS CARNOVSKY; *Victor Kranish,* PAUL CAVANAUGH; *Ethel Royce,* NATALIE SCHAFER; *District Attorney,* DOUGLAS DUMBRILLE; *Mrs. Geiger,* MARGARET HAMILTON; *Defense Attorney,* NICHOLAS JOY; *Detective,* JAMES FLAVIN; *Shirley,* RANSOM SHERMAN; *Jim,* DEWEY ROBINSON; *Plainclothesman,* ROBERT B. WILLIAMS

As Madeleine Damien

With Natalie Schafer

With Dennis O'Keefe

With Margaret Hamilton

SYNOPSIS

Unable to find any meaning to her life, Madeleine Damien, a magazine editor, attempts suicide. Dr. Caleb, a psychiatrist, rescues her and urges her to leave her job for new surroundings.

She changes her identity, moves to Greenwich Village, and takes up painting. There she meets David Cousins, a scientist. They plan to marry but are delayed when he is called out of the city.

During his absence, Madeleine goes to a nightclub. There she meets Felix Courtland, a wealthy jeweler with whom she had once been intimate. Courtland takes her to his home, but she slips out the rear door when he goes to the front door to answer the bell.

The caller is Jack Garet, who is employed by Courtland. Garet has stolen some jewels from Courtland and has come to plead with him not to notify the police.

Garet murders Courtland to silence him. Known as the last person to be with Courtland, Madeleine is arrested and tried for the crime.

David, shocked to learn of her past, will not see her. Despondent, Madeleine refuses to defend herself.

Dr. Caleb, believing her innocent, induces David to stand by her. His declaration of love prompts her to fight for her life. Through her testimony the evidence is resifted, and Courtland's house is searched. Police find fingerprints on the safe, and Garet confesses. Madeleine is exonerated, and she and David are reunited.

REVIEWS

SHOWMEN'S TRADE REVIEW

It is particularly good entertainment for the class houses where the more sophisticated audience may more thoroughly enjoy and understand this type of story. Miss Lamarr does a creditable job in the role of the young woman upset by internal conflicting emotions. As usual, she is very attractive to look at, and manages to convey her confusion convincingly.

VARIETY

This remake of the stage play has been weakened by censorship regulations but still has enough meat to attract femme audiences with proper exploitation. Production values are on the lavish side. Hedy Lamarr name figuring an aid in the selling. Hedy Lamarr character is more psychological than immoral and the film approach, because of taboos, lessens interest and clarity. Miss Lamarr's work is strong, nevertheless, and will help to carry the picture through to good grosses.

Miss Lamarr has bitten off quite a hunk of role here (Katharine Cornell played it on the Broadway stage), but, while she's no Cornell when it comes to acting, at least Hedy's a much better actress than she originally was.

MOTION PICTURE DAILY

Hedy Lamarr, Dennis O'Keefe, and John Loder are the marquee names provided by this Hunt Stromberg presentation, which recounts with full melodramatic emphasis the woeful story about a highly successful business woman whose long list of promiscuous love affairs, born of a bewildered seeking for pleasure, has brought her to grips with her conscience and to the brink of suicide. Miss Lamarr's presence plus the fact that Miss Lamarr and Loder are husband and wife in real life, are factors which combine to spell considerable box-office promise for this one . . . . Under the able direction of Robert Stevenson, they have made the characters they portray interesting at least —accomplishments which would be out of the reach of less experienced performers. . . . Jack Chertok's production is handsomely mounted and well fortified with excellent camera work.

NOTES

Hedy's second picture for her own producing company was high on technical values and low on just about everything else. Her performance is not a good one. She was poorly directed by Robert Stevenson, who must have been out to lunch during the filming. The result looks as if Miss Lamarr must have attempted to direct herself.

Her husband, John Loder, was killed off in the script before he could have much to do and was therefore wasted. Dennis O'Keefe was not a strong enough personality to complement Hedy in the romantic situations, which made dull watching for even the most undiscerning voyeur. Both Margaret Hamilton and Natalie Schafer essayed their particular brand of "camp," which pleases a peculiar type of audience.

LET'S LIVE A LITTLE

An Eagle-Lion Picture   (1948)
A United California Production

CREDITS

Directed by Richard Wallace. *Produced by* Eugene Frenke *and* Robert Cummings. *Screenplay by* Howard Irving Young, Edmund Hartmann, *and* Albert J. Cohen. *Based on an original story by* Albert J. Cohen *and* Jack Harvey. *Director of photography,* Ernest Laszlo. *Art direction by* Edward L. Ilou. *Set decoration by* Armor Marlowe *and* Robert P. Fox. *Costumes by* Elois Jenssen. *Makeup by* Ern Westmore *and* Joe Stinton. *Hair styles by* Joan St. Oegger *and* Helen Turpin. *Music by* Werner Heymann. *Musical direction by* Irving Friedman. *Special effects by* George J. Teague. *Recording directors,* Leon S. Becker *and* Howard J. Fogetti. *Film editor,* Arthur Hilton. *Running time, 85 minutes.*

CAST

Dr. J. O. Loring, HEDY LAMARR; *Duke Crawford,* ROBERT CUMMINGS; *Michele Bennett,* ANNA STEN; *Dr. Richard Field,* ROBERT SHAYNE; *Miss Adams,* MARY TREEN; *James Montgomery,* HARRY ANTRIM; *M. C.,* HAL K. DAWSON; *Morton,* BILLY BEVAN; *Chemist,* CURT BOIS; *Newcomb,* JOHN NEWLAND; *Lewis,* JIMMY DOBB; *Artist,* FRANK SULLY; *Photographer,* OLIVER BLAKE; *Dempster,* JOHN DEHNER; *Salesman,* FRANK WILCOX; *Miss O'Reilly,* EVE WHITNEY; *Cruickshank,* EDDIE PARKS; *Nurse Brady,* NORMA VARDEN; *Pierre,* LEO MOSTOVOY; *Sarah,* LILLIAN RANDOLPH; *Mrs. Harris,* VIRGINIA FARMER; *Mr. Stevens,* PAUL MAXEY; *Mr. Tinker,* LUCIEN LITTLEFIELD; *Mrs. Lansworth,* REGINA WALLACE; *Mr. Hopkins,* BYRON FOULGER

As Dr. Loring

With Norma Varden

With Robert Cummings

A scene from the dream sequence

SYNOPSIS

Duke Crawford, an advertising executive, is a nervous wreck because of Michele Bennett. She will renew his million-dollar contract only if Duke will continue their former love affair.

Because of his nervous condition, Duke is taken off Michele's account and assigned to promote a new book by Dr. J. O. Loring, a lady psychiatrist. His meeting with Dr. Loring ends in a consultation regarding his nervous condition.

She learns that Michele is the cause of his problems and suggests that he use a new tactic: He should take her out and give her a lot of attention.

Dr. Loring goes to a nightclub to observe the proceedings. Michele meets her and immediately suspects a more than patient-doctor relationship. She starts a fight, causing Duke to lose his nerve completely.

Dr. Loring takes him to the country for a complete rest; they fall in love. Later, Duke becomes furious when he overhears her describe him as a "guinea pig" in an experiment she is conducting.

He leaves her and goes back to Michele, who makes him agree to marry her before she will sign the contract. This so upsets Dr. Loring that she also becomes a nervous wreck. Everything is eventually straightened out, and Duke ends up with Dr. Loring in his arms.

REVIEWS

HOLLYWOOD REPORTER

Let's Live a Little is a moderately diverting romantic comedy whose laugh content is considerably higher in the opening scenes than it is as the action progresses. The script simply fails to take the fullest advantage of solid story premise. The production of Eugene Frenke and Robert Cummings is, however, pleasant enough to look at and the artful mugging of the principals goes a long way toward holding interest. If *Let's Live a Little* isn't altogether up to snuff, its giddy plot is not completely without merit and the not too discriminating filmgoer might reasonably find it much to his liking. . . . Hedy Lamarr, attractive as always, does an elegant job with her high comedy assignment, and Cummings works zealously as the advertising man.

LOS ANGELES TIMES

Starting with Robert Cummings, most of the players in *Let's Live a Little* fall victim to "frazzled nerves." This is a nice, simple phrase used in the comedy to describe the psychoneurotic fluctuations of the characters—particularly, again, of Mr. Cummings. I must say I found it all rather more amusing than a majority of the studio affairs being perpetrated these days in the name of comedy, Freud and "psychoanalysis." . . . Miss Lamarr is her customary self—vague, cool and bewitching.

PHOTOPLAY

Acting on the premise that all advertising executives are wacky and Robert Cummings is wackier than most, this provides Bob with a real slapstick role . . . . His nerves are so frazzled, he has to consult a psychiatrist—and who do you suppose said psychiatrist turns out to be? Hedy Lamarr! That clever little lady sets about curing Bob of his woman-hating phobia, only to fall for her—but hard. No use looking for logic or subtlety here; simply accept this as a moderately amusing movie and let it go at that.

With Robert Cummings, Leo Mostovoy, Robert Shayne and Anna Sten

NOTES

When Hedy was asked to appear in *Let's Live a Little*, she figured a comedy would be a good change of pace at the time. She enjoyed playing farce and showed a flair for it in *Comrade X.* The two dramas that she had made for her own company had been filmed through the facilities at the Goldwyn Studio in Hollywood, so she didn't have to go far to work on the new picture to be made by Eagle-Lion, a little company just around the corner from the Goldwyn complex.

The film turned out to be a silly comedy with Robert Cummings as her leading man. Cummings, who later made a fortune in television, had a long but undistinguished film career, his most memorable film being *Kings Row,* the classic picture in which he portrayed Parris Mitchell opposite Ann Sheridan. He was not a good partner for Hedy, and they did not work well together.

Let's Live a Little has little to commend it, the exceptions being Hedy Lamarr's mere presence of beauty and the camera work performed by Ernest Laszlo, one of Hollywood's greatest cinematographers, who was later responsible for making *Judgment at Nuremberg, Ship of Fools,* and *Airport* look brilliant.

With Robert Cummings

SAMSON AND DELILAH

A Paramount Picture   (1949)

With Victor Mature

CREDITS

Produced and directed by Cecil B. De Mille. *Screenplay by* Jesse Lasky, Jr., *and* Frederick M. Frank. *From original treatments by* Harold Lamb *and* Vladimir Jabotinsky. *Based on the history of Samson and Delilah in the Holy Bible,* Judges 13–16. *Director of photography,* George Barnes. *Director of photographic effects,* Gordon Jennings. *Unit directors,* Arthur Rosson *and* Ralph Jester. *Art direction by* Hans Dreier *and* Walter Tyler. *Set decoration by* Sam Comer *and* Ray Moyer. *Costumes by* Edith Head, Dorothy Jeakins, Elois Jenssen, Gile Steele, *and* Gwen Wakeling. *Music by* Victor Young. *Sound recording by* Harry Lindgren *and* John Cope. *Makeup by* Wally Westmore. *Choreography by* Theodore Kosloff. *Film editor,* Anne Bauchens. *Process photography by* Farciot Edouart *and* Wallace Kelley. *Holy Land photography by* Dewey Wrigley. *Filmed in Technicolor. Running time, 131 minutes.*

CAST

Delilah, HEDY LAMARR; *Samson,* VICTOR MATURE; *The Saran of Gaza,* GEORGE SANDERS; *Semadar,* ANGELA LANSBURY; *Ahtur,* HENRY WILCOXON; *Miriam,* OLIVE DEERING; *Hazeleponit,* FAY HOLDEN; *Hisham,* JULIA FAYE; *Saul,* RUSTY(RUSS) TAMBLYN; *Tubal,* WILLIAM FARNUM: *Teresh,* LANE CHANDLER; *Targil,* MORONI OLSEN; *Storyteller,* FRANCIS J. McDONALD; *Garmishkar,* WILLIAM DAVIS; *Lesh Lakish,* JOHN MILJAN; *Fat Philistine Merchant,* ARTHUR Q. BRYAN; *Spectators,* LAURA ELLIOT, DOROTHY ADAMS, JEFF YORK; *Lord of Ashdod,* VICTOR VARCONI; *Lord of Gath,* JOHN PARRISH; *Lord of Ekron,* FRANK WILCOX; *Lord of Ashkelon,* RUSSELL HICKS; *Prince,* NILS ASTHER; *Lord Sharif,* FRITZ LEIBER; *Woman,* KAREN MORLEY; *Bar Simon,* PEDRO de CORDOBA; *Wounded Messenger,* GEORGE REEVES; *Leader of Philistine Soldiers,* MIKE MAZURKI; *Prince,* COLIN TAPLEY; *First Priest,* BOYD DAVIS; *Merchant Prince,* DAVISON CLARK; *Village Barber,* FRANK REICHER; *Manoah, Samson's Father,* CHARLES EVANS; *Saran's Chariot Driver,* HENRY WILLS; *Danite Merchant,* CHARLES JUDELS; *Priests,* PIERRE WATKIN, FRED GRAHAM; *Court Astrologer,* CRAUFORD KENT; *Gammad,* HARRY WOODS; *Chief Scribe,* LLOYD WHITLOCK; *Bergam,* STEPHEN ROBERTS; *Prince,* JAMES CRAVEN; *Gristmill Captain,* TOM TYLER; *Spectators,* MARGARET FIELD, JOHN KELLOGG; *Makon,* ED HINTON; *Overseer at Gristmill,* RAY BENNETT

As Delilah

SYNOPSIS

The time is 1100 B.C., and the place is the land of Dan. The Danites, held in subjugation by the Philistines, look to a young shepherd of massive strength, Samson, to free them from tyranny.

By a feat of great courage, Samson kills a lion with his bare hands. Because of his bravery, the Saran of Gaza, leader of the Philistines, consents to his marrying a Philistine woman, Semadar. Through the treachery of Semadar's sister, the seductive Delilah, he loses Semadar to a Philistine warrior. Delilah wants Samson for herself. She is offered as a substitute for Samadar, but Samson rejects her.

A riot ensues; during the melee, Semadar is killed. Samson flees. Her home demolished, her sister and father dead, Delilah vows to destroy Samson. She soon becomes a favorite of the Saran.

Delilah sets out to trap Samson. She works her wiles, wins his love, and then betrays him. Believing his great strength comes from his hair, Delilah drugs him and shears his head. The Philistines capture Samson but promise Delilah no blade will touch his skin.

With Victor Mature

(ABOVE LEFT) With
Henry Wills, George
Sanders, Angela
Lansbury, Henry
Wilcoxen and Victor
Mature

They blind him by holding a red-hot poker to his eyes. Samson is chained and tortured, then brought to the temple where the Philistines intend to force him to bow before their fiery idol.

Delilah is horrified at the sight of Samson blinded, helpless. Saddened by what she has done, she goes to him, pretends to take part in his torment, and tells him of her love for him. He asks her to lead him to the columns that support the temple. His mighty strength returns; he loosens the columns and causes the temple to crash down on his enemies and on Delilah and himself as well.

REVIEWS

HOLLYWOOD REPORTER

Samson and Delilah is an old-fashioned epic, and we use the description "old-fashioned" with deepest respect. For we are not inclined to the theory that sound entertainment values change with the spinning of the clock or to the tune of a Hollywood cycle. The Biblical motion picture pageant as pioneered by Cecil B. De Mille holds a unique position in boxoffice annals, and there is every reason to believe that his newest effort from the Testament will carry on in the same fine tradition. . . .*Samson and Delilah* is all the more fascinating because such a picture comes only once in a decade. . . . The picture has everything—passion, love, hate, tremendous pageantry, color production and, certainly, entertainment. There isn't a dull moment in its running time, thanks to the majesty of De Mille's presentation. . . . The Delilah of Hedy Lamarr is just the role for the sultry, dark-haired beauty. The Technicolor camera gives her every possible advantage, and her acting of the famous siren is everything that it should be.

LOOK

His (De Mille) Technicolor *Samson and Delilah,* for Paramount, surges across the screen with colossal scenes of spectacle, violence, passion-in-the-desert, woman's treachery—and retribution to sinners. The De Mille brand of showmanship may seem a little old-fashioned in 1950. But it still towers, after his 36 years of hits, and marks him as the most serenely individualistic creative money-maker remaining at work in the movies. Victor Mature and Hedy Lamarr have the title roles of *Samson and Delilah.* Mature is probably the only actor in the world who could make Samson's strong-man exploits so believable. And Miss Lamarr puts across the fabled allure of Delilah, one of history's most neurotic female sadists.

With Victor Mature

The famous peacock dress

COLLIER'S

Already certain other producers, who should know, are predicting that *Samson and Delilah* will outstrip the modern title holder, *Gone with the Wind*.

FILM BULLETIN

The casting of Hedy Lamarr and Victor Mature in the title roles was inspired. Physically, they are the very prototypes of the Bible characters, and their performances rank with the best they have ever given.

SHOWMEN'S TRADE REVIEW

For this famous couple, Victor Mature and Hedy Lamarr are ideal choices. . . . Miss Lamarr is just about everyone's conception of the fair-skinned, dark-haired, beauteous Delilah, a role tailor-made for her, and her best acting chore to date.

NOTES

Samson and Delilah was a blockbuster due mainly to the casting of Hedy Lamarr in the central part. It was the high point of her career, and she scored a triumph. She was magnificent as she connived and clawed her way through the Technicolor epic. It was unforgivable that Academy members did not see fit to bestow a nomination on her for her grand job. No other film actress of the day could have done justice to Delilah as did Miss Lamarr. It was a miracle that De Mille chose Hedy at all since he even considered Betty Hutton for the part. He was not always a good judge in the casting department, as the choice of Angela Lansbury as Hedy's sister bears out. For Samson to have desired Lansbury over the gorgeous Lamarr, he would have had to be blinded in the first reel.

Samson and Delilah is one of the all-time box-office champs and won two Academy Awards: best art direction; best costume design. It also received nominations for cinematography, music score, and special effects.

A LADY WITHOUT PASSPORT

A Metro-Goldwyn-Mayer Picture   (1950)

CREDITS

Directed by Joseph H. Lewis. *Produced by* Samuel Marx. *Screenplay by* Howard Dimsdale. *Adaptation by* Cyril Hume. *Suggested story by* Lawrence Taylor. *Director of photography,* Paul C. Vogel. *Art direction by* Cedric Gibbons *and* Edward Carfagno. *Music by* David Raksin. *Film editor,* Frederick Y. Smith. *Running time: 72 minutes.*

CAST

Marianne Lorress, HEDY LAMARR; *Pete Karezag,* JOHN HODIAK; *Frank Westlake,* JAMES CRAIG; *Palinov,* GEORGE MACREADY; *Frenchman,* STEVEN GERAY; *Archer Delby James,* BRUCE COWLING; *Harry Nordell,* NEDERICK YOUNG; *Jack,* STEVEN HILL; *Lt. Lannahan,* ROBERT OSTERLOH; *Lt. Carfagno,* TREVOR BARDETTE; *Beryl Sandring,* ESTHER ZEITLIN; *Mr. Sandring,* CARLO TRICOLI; *Navy Flyer,* RICHARD CRANE; *Dancer,* NITA BIEBER; *Police Officer,* MARTIN GARRALAGA; *Cafe Owner,* MARIO SILETTI

SYNOPSIS

An immigration inspector, Pete Karezag, poses as a refugee seeking admittance into the United States. He is trying to get evidence against a man named Palinov, the leader of an alien smuggling ring.

He contacts Palinov in Havana. Through Palinov, Pete meets a beautiful refugee, Marianne Lorress, with whom he falls in love. This does not set well with Palinov, who wants Marianne for himself. Before long, Palinov discovers Pete's true identity.

With that information, Palinov turns Marianne against Pete. He tells her that Pete is using her as a dupe. She refuses Pete's proposal of marriage, which would automatically make her an American citizen. Instead, she joins Palinov's party of aliens on an illegal flight to the United States.

As Marianne Lorress   With John Hodiak

Opposite page (top) With Martin Garralaga and John Hodiak

Pete alerts officials about the flight, and navy planes set out on a search. Discovering a plane on his tail, Palinov crashes in the Florida Everglades. Pete heads for the landing site. He finally catches up with Palinov, outwits him, and rescues Marianne.

She realizes that she was wrong to enter the country illegally and prepares to pay the penalty. With this in mind, she looks forward to the day when she and Pete will be reconciled.

With George Macready and Bruce Cowling

REVIEWS

VARIETY

Beginning is a bit too cryptic for quick understanding, but when plot line does take shape, the story builds and holds attention. Joseph H. Lewis' direction spins it along expertly, neatly pacing the suspenseful sequences. . . . Miss Lamarr and Hodiak carry off their assignments excellently, and Macready turns in another of his good heavies.

FILM BULLETIN

This romantic meller from Metro is rather routine stuff. There are some suspenseful moments, but the plot is of the programmer variety that will satisfy only avid action fans. . . . The performances are not noteworthy. The beauty and acting ability of Miss Lamarr are almost completely wasted in the role of the lady in the title.

THE NEW YORK TIMES

Undoubtedly *A Lady Without Passport* is meant as a tribute to the self-effacing stalwarts of the U.S. Immigration and Naturalization Service. But the comparatively tiny group of guardians of our far-flung boundaries has to compete with pulp-fiction romance and adventure. The competition is too tough. . . . As Marianne Lorress, the misused dame whose trials include a stretch in Buchenwald, Hedy Lamarr is beautiful and wears her clothes exceedingly well.

SHOWMEN'S TRADE REVIEW

There's nothing here to offend anyone, nor to excite anyone particularly, but it's a pleasant enough little film. . . . There's a strong possibility that this cast was wasted on a film of this type. . . . Apart from the cast, which does well in familiar roles, the film is little more than extra strong supporting fare.

Opposite page (below left) Studying her script on the set

Opposite page (below right) With John Hodiak and George Macready

With George Macready and John Hodiak

NOTES

Back on the MGM lot for the first time in five years, Hedy had the unfortunate experience of being cast in *A Lady Without Passport*. Some welcome-home present! It turned out to be a programmer that couldn't be lifted out of the B category and quite often ended up as the lower half of a double bill.

The biggest mistake of the picture, which had the working title of *Visa,* was the casting of John Hodiak, a competent but boring actor, in the major role of the immigration inspector. An actor of stronger sex appeal, such as Robert Mitchum or John Garfield, was needed to stir Hedy's passions in the hot climate of the Cuban capital.

This was the type of film Columbia didn't make any better but somehow had greater success with, when they presented Rita Hayworth in *Gilda* and *An Affair in Trinidad.*

With Maxine Gates, Hope Emerson and Robert Watson

COPPER CANYON
A Paramount Picture   (1950)

CREDITS

Directed by John Farrow. *Produced by* Mel Epstein. *Screenplay by* Jonathan Latimer. *Based on a story by* Richard English. *Director of photography,* Charles B. Lang, Jr. *Art direction by* Hans Dreier and Franz Bachelin. *Costumes by* Edith Head. *Music by* Daniele Amfitheatrof. *Song by* Jay Livingston and Ray Evans. *Recording directors,* Harold Lewis and Gene Garvin. *Film editor,* Eda Warren. *Filmed in Technicolor. Running time, 83 minutes.*

As Lisa Roselle

CAST

Johnny Carter, RAY MILLAND; *Lisa Roselle,* HEDY LAMARR; *Lane Travis,* MACDONALD CAREY; *Caroline Desmond,* MONA FREEMAN; *Lt. Ord,* HARRY CAREY, JR.; *Mullins,* FRANK FAYLEN; *Ma Tarbet,* HOPE EMERSON; *Theodosius Roberts,* TAYLOR HOLMES; *Cora,* PEGGY KNUDSEN; *Jeb Bassett,* JAMES BURKE; *Scamper,* PERCY HELTON; *Sheriff Wattling,* PHILIP VAN ZANDT; *Moss Balfour,* FRANCIS PIERLOT; *Professor,* ERNO VEREBES; *Bat Laverne,* PAUL LEES; *Bixby,* ROBERT WATSON; *Martha Bassett,* GEORGIA BACKUS; *Mr. Henderson,* IAN WOLFE; *Blonde Dancer,* MAXINE GATES; *Bartender,* LEN HENDRY; *Lew Partridge,* BUDDY ROOSEVELT; *Proprietor's Wife,* JULIA FAYE; *Proprietor,* JOE WHITHEAD; *Southerner,* REX LEASE; *Bartender,* STANLEY ANDREWS

With Macdonald Carey and Ray Milland

SYNOPSIS

Former Confederates seek to make their fortunes in Coppertown and are driven against the wall by ruthless Northerners who own the only smelter around. They will only buy the Southerners' ore on their terms.

The Southerners seek help from Johnny Carter, a trickshot performer whom they believe to be a Confederate hero. He arrives with a troupe in Coppertown and immediately sets out to charm Lisa Roselle, owner of a saloon, much to the chagrin of Lane Travis, the crooked deputy sheriff.

Johnny secretly joins the small-mine owners in a plan to send their ore thirty miles away to another smelter. Travis has been able to block this so far. Hearing of the plan from a spy, he calls on Lisa to help stop Johnny from leading the wagon train full of ore. Lisa, who has been part of the conspiracy against the Southerners, fails in her attempt to get Johnny drunk.

As a masked rider, Johnny breaks up an attempt by Travis and his men to wreck the wagon train. Travis steals the Southerners' profits from the sale of the ore, frames Johnny, and jails him for robbery.

By now, Lisa has fallen in love with Johnny and has become sick of Travis's murderous acts. She bribes the jailer to free him.

Johnny rounds up the small-mine owners, and in an ensuing attack, Travis is killed. With the small-mine owners sure of a fair deal, Johnny and Lisa leave Coppertown together to start a new life.

REVIEWS

MOTION PICTURE DAILY

A top-notch outdoor action drama in Technicolor is offered in *Copper Canyon.* A strong cast, headed by Ray Milland, Hedy Lamarr, and Macdonald Carey, is supported by an impressive production frame.

With Ray Milland

LOS ANGELES TIMES

Miss Lamarr switches to a new province, wears just as attractive garb as in any other film. She is the boss of a gambling establishment, and attires herself as femininely as you please, and alluringly. She and Milland don't mince matters about their love scenes, although these are not superabundant. She is well set off in the picture, and gives a pleasing performance.

LOS ANGELES EXAMINER

Pictorially, everything is just plain gorgeous in Technicolor, aided by the pictorial natural grandeur of Arizona (where it was filmed) pitch-hitting for Nevada for reasons best known to location scouts. . . . It should come as no surprise that Hedy Lamarr looks beautiful in her adventuress rags and emotes with zest.

With Macdonald Carey and Ray Milland

SHOWMEN'S TRADE REVIEW

Off the beaten track of even "super-westerns," this outdoor film, beautifully photographed in Technicolor, arouses audience interest from the start, and the action never lets the interest lag. There's action for the western fans; the story and acting for those who demand something more. The production of Mel Epstein, the direction of John Farrow and the performances of the principals are right out of the top drawer. . . . The beautiful Hedy Lamarr gives a pleasing performance, though a little more fire would have heightened her importance to the story.

With Macdonald Carey

NOTES

Copper Canyon is no better or worse than the run-of-the-mill Westerns being churned out by every studio at the time. Director John Farrow managed to keep the action going even though he had difficulty with Ray Milland, who was miscast in the role of a fast-gun hero. Of all people! The script by Jonathan Latimer was at least competent, Edith Head's costumes handsome, and cameraman Charles B. Lang, Jr.'s, lush color photography was first-rate.

Hedy said she enjoyed working with Ray Milland. Milland, on the other hand, has been quoted in an interview as saying, "*Copper Canyon* I loathed. I hated working with Hedy Lamarr." An ungallant remark from this actor should not perturb Miss Lamarr, for in his autobiography, Milland also takes swipes at several other of his peers, such as Marlene Dietrich, Hedda Hopper, and Lord Olivier.

With Bob Hope

MY FAVORITE SPY

A Paramount Picture   (1951)

CREDITS

Directed by Norman Z. McLeod. Produced by Paul Jones. Screenplay by Edmund Hartmann and Jack Sher. Additional dialogue by Hal Kanter. Story and adaptation by Edmund Beloin and Lou Breslow. Director of photography, Victor Milner. Film editor, Frank Bracht. Costumes by Edith Head. Music by Victor Young. Song, "I Wind Up Taking a Fall," by Johnny Mercer and Robert Emmett Dolan. Song, "Just a Moment More," by Jay Livingston and Ray Evans. Running time, 93 minutes.

CAST

Peanuts White/Eric Augustine, BOB HOPE; *Lily Dalbray,* HEDY LAMARR; *Karl Brubaker,* FRANCIS L. SULLIVAN; *Tasso,* ARNOLD MOSS; *Harry Crock,* TONIO SELWART; *Donald Bailey,* STEPHEN CHASE; *Henderson,* JOHN ARCHER; *Gen. Fraser,* MORRIS ANKRUM; *Ben Ali,* MARC LAWRENCE; *Lola,* IRIS ADRIAN; *Hoenig,* LUIS VAN ROOTEN; *Monkara,* MIKE MAZURKI; *El Sarif,* RALPH SMILEY

As Lily Dalbray

With Bob Hope and
Francis L. Sullivan

With Bob Hope

SYNOPSIS

Eric Augustine, a foreign spy who is the only link to a German scientist who possesses a piece of microfilm containing a short cut to the hydrogen bomb, is cornered by government agents on the eve of his departure for Tangier. He manages to elude capture.

Peanuts White, a burlesque comic who looks exactly like Augustine, is picked up by the police, who mistake him for the spy. When the real spy is captured, officials induce Peanuts to pose as Augustine and go to Tangier to contact the scientist and buy the microfilm.

Arriving in Tangier, Peanuts finds himself involved with a lovely singer, Lily Dalbray, Augustine's sweetheart. She is a member of an international spy ring headed by Karl Brubaker.

Peanuts meets the scientist and obtains the microfilm. But he soon finds himself plagued by Brubaker, who is determined to acquire the film.

Matters become more complicated when Augustine, who has escaped, arrives in Tangier. After many mix-ups, during which Augustine is killed, Peanuts confesses his masquerade to Lily.

She joins forces with him and helps him save the microfilm and bring about the arrest of Brubaker. The government promises Peanuts $10,000, which he and Lily will use to open a haberdashery in New Jersey.

REVIEWS

FILM BULLETIN

My Favorite Spy is a Bob Hope comedy that rides high from start to finish and is destined to do the same for the boxoffice. The script is a bit of zany writing neatly tailored to Hope's specifications, packed with solid laugh lines and situations that afford the funny man opportunity to indulge himself in everything from satire to slapstick. With Hedy Lamarr as his sultry vis-à-vis, the romantics are wildly insane, and both stars deliver in the grand manner.

HOLLYWOOD REPORTER

My Favorite Spy, with its giddy story of a burlesque comic who impersonates an international charlatan, is tip-top Bob Hope fare, a rollicking, zany comedy that affords Hope ample opportunity to unfurl his versatile bag of tricks. . . . And, of course, as a sultry siren of international intrigue, Hedy Lamarr is a delight to the eye and just the foil Hope needs to enliven the romantics.

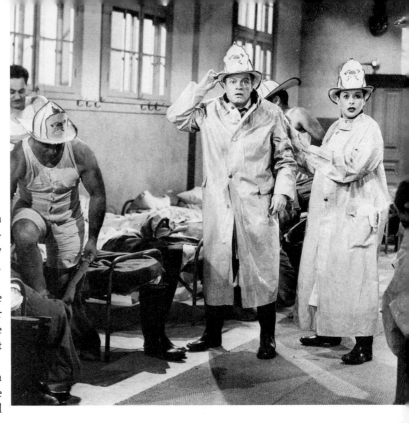

HOLLYWOOD CITIZEN-NEWS

Spell the name Bob Hope and the object of his affections, Hedy Lamarr, and you have a combination that tickles the funnybone no end in Paramount's lively new comedy, *My Favorite Spy*. . . . The final chase sequence, when Hope tries to escape the villains, is a knockout. With Hedy driving a hook-and-ladder fire engine, and Hope swinging perilously from the top, this chase is mighty amusing stuff.

NOTES

Sometime ago, there was a newspaper columnist who often featured a line called: Don't Invite 'Ems. This meant, don't invite two celebrities who detest each other to the same party. This can be said of Miss Lamarr and Bob Hope. She says the comedian pruned some of her best scenes from *My Favorite Spy*. Because of that, she has disliked him ever since.

It seems the lady was able to pull off a most difficult feat; stealing a movie from Hope. However, one of her funniest scenes was allowed to remain. The idea of the beauteous Lamarr, wearing a fireman's slicker and hat, driving a fire engine at breakneck speed through a North African city, is hilarious. That is much funnier than Hope swinging in the breeze from a ladder high above it, which is something one expects of him.

As an international spy doubling as a cabaret entertainer, Hedy sang "Just a Moment More." Although Paramount said her voice was not dubbed, it is obvious that it was. Her lip synchronization of both the English and French lyrics was perfect, but the voice did not even resemble that of Hedy's.

As Helen of Troy

ETERNA FEMMINA
ETERNAL WOMAN
Also known as
L'AMANTE DI PARIDE
THE LOVE OF THREE
QUEENS

A Cino Del Duca—P.C.E. Production   (Italo-French, 1954)

CREDITS

Directed by Marc Allegret and Edgar Ulmer. *Produced by* Victor Pahlen. *Script by* Nino Novarese, Marc Allegret, and Salka Viertel. *Based on a story by* Aeneas Mackenzie, Marc Allegret, and Vadim Plenianikoy. *Dialogue by* Aeneas Mackenzie and Hugh Gray. *Photography by* Desmond Dickinson and Fernando Risi. *Art direction by* Virgilio Marchi and Mario Chiari. *Music by* Nino Rota. *Recording director,* K. Dubrawsky. *Film editor,* Manuel Del Campo. *Filmed in Technicolor.*

CAST

Hedy Windsor; Helen of Troy; Empress Josephine; Genieve de Brabant, HEDY LAMARR;   *Napoleon Bonaparte,* GERARD OURY; *Paris,* MASSIMO SERATO; *Menelaus,* ROBERT BEATTY; *Oenone,* CATHY O'DONNELL; *Jupiter,* GUIDO CELANO; *Priamus,* ENRICO GLORI; *Cassandra,* SEREN MICHELOTTI; *Venus,* ALBA ARNOVA; *and* TERENCE MORGAN, CAESAR DANOVA.

SYNOPSIS

Beautiful socialite Hedy Windsor receives an invitation to the event of the season. It is a masked ball, and she must decide on a costume. She believes that the selection should be from the list of history's most celebrated women. It must be a personality that most closely reflects her own refined personality.

Three admirers put before her three suggestions: She is seen by the first as the sweet, beloved Genieve de Brabant; the second sees Hedy as the intelligent and fascinating Josephine de Beauharnais, Napoleon's elegant empress; the third believes the personality most comparable to Hedy's is Helen of Troy.

Hedy conjures up each of the three characters in her imagination but cannot convince herself that she is like any of the three. She will not go to the ball as any of the three personalities. She must think of another characterization that will suit her better.

Each woman and all women are the same and different, endowed with one unchangeable face and with a hundred contrasting faces. All women are Woman, the Eterna Femmina.

With Robert Beatty

As Genieve de Brabant

With Massimo Serato

NOTES

This spaghetti epic had so many titles during and after the filming that it has often been thought that Hedy had made more than one film at that time. Called *Eterna Femmina* when first shown in Italy, it has been shown on American television as *The Love of Three Queens*.

Miss Lamarr formed her own company to make the film and shot it on location in Montegelato, Italy. The expense involved in such a massive undertaking was staggering, and everyone involved lost a great amount of money. The picture, which originally ran over three hours, had only a limited release in Europe and was never shown theatrically in the United States.

THE STORY OF MANKIND

A Warner Bros. Picture   (1957)

CREDITS

Produced and directed by Irwin Allen. *Associate producer,* George E. Swink. *Screenplay by* Irwin Allen and Charles Bennett. *Based on the book by* Hendrik van Loon. *Director of photography,* Nick Musuraca. *Filmed in Technicolor. Art direction by* Art Loel. *Costumes by* Majorie Best. *Editor,* Gene Palmer. *Supervising film editor,* Ronald Gross. *Music composed and conducted by* Paul Sawtell. *Running time, 100 minutes.*

CAST

Spirit of Man, RONALD COLMAN; *Joan of Arc,* HEDY LAMARR; *Peter Minuit,* GROUCHO MARX; *Isaac Newton,* HARPO MARX; *Monk,* CHICO MARX; *Cleopatra,* VIRGINIA MAYO; *Queen Elizabeth,* AGNES MOOREHEAD; *The Devil,* VINCENT PRICE; *Nero,* PETER LORRE; *Hippocrates,* CHARLES COBURN; *High Judge,* CEDRIC HARDWICKE; *Spanish Envoy,* CESAR ROMERO; *Khufu,* JOHN CARRADINE; *Napoleon,* DENNIS HOPPER; *Marie Antoinette,* MARIE WILSON; *Mark Antony,* HELMUT DANTINE; *Sir Walter Raleigh,* EDWARD EVERETT HORTON; *Shakespeare,* REGINALD GARDINER; *Josephine,* MARIE WINDSOR; *Early Christian Woman,* CATHY O'DONNELL; *Moses,* FRANCIS X. BUSHMAN; *Alexander Graham Bell,* JIM AMECHE; *Adolf Hitler,* BOBBY WATSON; *Columbus,* ANTHONY DEXTER; *Cleopatra's Brother,* BART MATTSON; *Helen of Troy,* DANI CRAYNE; *Laughing Water,* EDEN HARTFORD; *Marquis de Varennes,* FRANKLIN PANGBORN; *Waiter,* GEORGE E. STONE; *Major Domo,* MELVILLE COOPER; *Apprentice,* NICK CRAVAT; *Bishop of Beauvais,* HENRY DANIELL; *Concubine,* ZIVA RODAAN; *Abraham Lincoln,* AUSTIN GREEN; *Indian Brave,* HARRY RUBY; *Julius Caesar,* REGINALD SCHALLERT; *Indian Chief,* ABRAHAM SOFAER; *Armana,* MARVIN MILLER; *Court Clerk,* TUDOR OWEN; *Early Christian Child,* MELINDA MARX.

As Joan of Arc

SYNOPSIS

A high tribunal in Heaven learns of the invention of a super H-bomb. All mankind would be ended if the bomb were detonated. The Spirit of Man, in defense of mankind, and the Devil, as his adversary, argue before the tribunal whether or not to allow the explosion of the bomb.

A series of flashbacks depicts historical events as each presents his argument and makes his point.

We are reminded of the greed and selfishness of the Egyptian Pharaohs; the Battle of Troy; the Golden Age of Greece; Cleopatra's affairs; Nero's debauchery and the burning of Rome; the early Christians' faith; the Dark Ages; King John and the Magna Carta; the triumph and tragedy of Joan of Arc; the conquests of Christopher Columbus and Hernando Cortez; the reign of Elizabeth I; the purchase of Manhattan Island from the Indians; Napoleon's downfall at Waterloo; the War of 1812; Bell's invention of the telephone and the invention of the electric light and airplane; World War I; Adolf Hitler and his Third Reich; and the development of the atom bomb.

The Tribunal decides to reserve its decision until another time. In the end, its members warn that the future of mankind depends on mankind itself.

REVIEWS

CHRISTIAN SCIENCE MONITOR

Leaving aside, however, the limitations of the story's presentation, the theme is timely, and it provides a lively and dramatic rendering of the more violent moments in "the story of mankind." Historical accuracy suffers somewhat in the process. . . . Hedy Lamarr as Joan of Arc, Marie Wilson as Marie Antoinette, Virginia Mayo as Cleopatra, Reginald Gardiner as Shakespeare, are a few of the stars seen briefly, and sometimes in bizarre casting, in the flashbacks.

VARIETY

Best of the portrayals is Agnes Moorehead's handling of the role of Queen Elizabeth and Cedric Hardwicke turns in a good performance as the High Judge. . . . Hedy Lamarr is miscast as Joan (yes, of Arc) in one of the few other key parts.

FILMS AND FILMING

Hendrik Van Loon's work, *The Story of Mankind*, was a brilliant piece of social history presented in a "popular science" format. The film is far from brilliant, presented as it is like all-too-popular Hollywood. . . . A collector's piece for those who like spotting the great with their hair-down, or who wish to join the game of spotting footage borrowed from such earlier Warner spectacles as *Helen of Troy* and *Land of the Pharaohs.*

MOTION PICTURE DAILY

The picture goes in for some unusual casting as witness Hedy Lamarr as Joan of Arc, Marie Wilson as Marie Antoinette, Charles Coburn as Hippocrates, Harpo Marx as Isaac Newton and Groucho Marx as Peter Minuit. Some of the famous moments shown include Nero's (Peter Lorre) musical interlude while Rome burns, the buying of Manhattan Island for twenty four dollars, Marie Antoinette's legendary "Let 'em eat cake," the burning of Joan of Arc, ad infinitum. . . . The cast and the very boldness of the venture should lure many patrons. The picture is unavoidably episodic and a guessing game as to who plays whom, but it is diverting in its capsule treatment of history.

NOTES

Did the producers expect anyone to take this flotsam seriously? The outrageous casting was ridiculous: Marie Wilson as Marie Antoinette! Dennis Hopper as Napoleon! Harpo Marx as Isaac Newton! Radio announcer Jim Ameche, instead of his brother Don, was cast as Alexander Graham Bell in what was probably meant to be an ingenious casting coup. Ronald Colman and Miss Lamarr were important stars who should not have gotten themselves involved in such a mess.

If it was made to be intentionally funny, then it failed miserably. Nobody knew just what it was. If it were made today, the possibilities in the hands of somebody like Mel Brooks would be limitless. They used to hand out special glasses for 3-D movies. They should have handed out clothespins with this picture.

THE FEMALE ANIMAL

A Universal-International Picture   (1957)

With George Nader

With Jan Sterling

CREDITS

Directed by Harry Keller. *Produced by* Albert Zugsmith. *Screenplay by* Robert Hill. *Based on a story by* Albert Zugsmith. *Director of photography,* Russell Metty. *Art direction by* Alexander Golitzen and Robert Clatworthy. *Set decoration by* Russell A. Gausman and Ruby R. Levitt. *Gowns by* Bill Thomas. *Music by* Hans J. Salter. *Music supervision by* Joseph Gershenson. *Recording directors,* Leslie I. Carey and Frank Wilkinson. *Film editor,* Milton Carruth. *Makeup by* Bud Westmore. *Running time, 92 minutes.*

CAST

Vanessa Windsor, HEDY LAMARR; *Penny Windsor,* JANE POWELL; *Chris Farley,* GEORGE NADER; *Lily Frayne,* JAN STERLING; *Hank Lopez,* JERRY PARIS; *Piggy,* GREGG PALMER; *Irma Jones,* MABEL ALBERTSON; *Tom Maloney,* JAMES GLEASON; *Charlie Grant,* CASEY ADAMS; *Nurse,* ANN DORAN; *Dr. John Ramsay,* RICHARD CUTTING; *Hairdresser,* YVONNE PEATTIE; *Landlady,* ALMIRA SESSIONS; *Movie Director,* DOUGLAS EVANS; *Mischa Boroff,* ARAM KATCHER; *Masseuse,* ISABEL DAWN; *Lily's Gigolo,* RICHARD AVONDE; *Manicurist,* LAURIE MITCHELL; *Movie Assistant Director,* WALTER KELLEY; *Coffee-wagon Attendant,* BOB WEGNER

SYNOPSIS

Chris Farley, a Hollywood extra, saves glamorous movie star Vanessa Windsor from a serious accident. She falls in love with him and persuades him to become caretaker of her beach house. One night, Chris meets a girl named Penny and takes her to the beach house, not knowing that she is Vanessa's adopted daughter.

As Vanessa Windsor

With George Nader

A few nights later, Vanessa and Chris meet another famous star, Lily Frayne, and Pepe, her gigolo boy friend. Lily's outspoken remarks make Chris realize that he is regarded as just another Pepe. He leaves abruptly, but Vanessa follows and tells him of her need for him.

Some days later, Penny tells Chris that she is Vanessa's daughter. Understanding one another's problems, a mutual attraction develops.

Penny returns to her mother's house and tells Vanessa of her feelings for Chris. Vanessa cannot bear to lose him. Hoping to hold him, she tells a gossip columnist that she and Chris plan to marry.

Furious, Chris returns to his old apartment. Vanessa finds him and begs him to give marriage a try. Upset and drunk, she attempts to do a dangerous scene in her movie. Chris and Penny watch nervously as she slips and falls into a pool on the set. Chris saves her once again.

She regains consciousness and realizes, finally, that Chris and Penny are in love. Vanessa renounces him in favor of her daughter's happiness.

REVIEWS

HOLLYWOOD REPORTER

U-I has a good glamour melodrama in *The Female Animal*. . . . Hill's screenplay has more than the expected quota of sharp and sometimes witty lines. The scenes and situations are capably composed for mounting interest and excitement and the motion picture business is accurately and interestingly presented. Miss Lamarr does an adequate job although some of the aspects of the character do not seem to get their full showing at times.

VARIETY

Miss Lamarr manages some semblance of reality as the star who seems half lit through most of the film, but George Nader as the extra suffers from lack of definitive character opportunity. Direction by Harry Keller seldom rises above the script, which generally affects various characters. Miss Powell overplays her opening drunk sequence and fares little better later on, although she fills a bathing suit with eye-filling allure.

FILM DAILY

The joys, anguish and complexities of love of a celebrated Hollywood star who has begun to reach her declining years are recounted with candor and dramatic excitement in *The Female Animal*. . . . Its cast is a splendid one that includes Hedy Lamarr, as the aging star.

NOTES

The Female Animal was Hedy's last film before her voluntary retirement from filmmaking. It was not a successful picture but one that she managed to hold together by giving a good performance despite little help from her coplayers. Again, the leading man should have been played by someone with more magnetism than George Nader. Jane Powell was not good, and Jan Sterling, who did act well, was not too believable as a glamorous star. Even a lesser actress such as Zsa Zsa Gabor would have been better typecast for the part.

SHORT SUBJECTS & FEATURE FILM CLIPS

Hedy's entrance in WHITE CARGO as she utters, "I am Tondeleyo." The clip was used in SOME OF THE BEST and THAT'S ENTERTAINMENT, 2

SCREEN SNAPSHOTS
Series 18, No. 10
Columbia (1939)

A charity ball sponsored by Mrs. Basil Rathbone on the Rathbones' Bel-Air estate. Shown first are preparations for the affair, in which many screen stars participate, including Hedy Lamarr, Dolores Del Rio and Claire Trevor. The affair itself is attended by practically all well-known film personages, who are filmed on arrival, at their tables and while dancing. Running time, 10 minutes.

SHOW BUSINESS AT WAR
Volume IX, Issue # 10 of "The March of Time"
20th Century-Fox (1943)

Directed by Louis de Rochemont. Produced by the editors of Time. Many Hollywood luminaries are seen participating in the war effort. Hedy Lamarr was shown on one of the many bond tours in which she took part. Among the other stars appearing were such names as Bing Crosby, Bette Davis, Olivia de Havilland, Marlene Dietrich, Deanna Durbin, Kay Francis, Clark Gable, Rita Hayworth, Lily Pons, Tyrone Power, Ginger Rogers, Ginny Simms, Frank Sinatra and Loretta Young. Running time, 18 minutes.

SOME OF THE BEST
Metro-Goldwyn-Mayer (1949)

A featurette commemorating MGM's Silver Anniversary. Hedy Lamarr was seen briefly in a scene from White Cargo. Other highlights included scenes from Metro's best films of the past; e.g. Meet Me in St. Louis, Mrs. Miniver, San Francisco, Grand Hotel and Boom Town. Included also were clips from the studio's current pictures, such as Little Women and The Stratton Story (both starring June Allyson), Madame Bovary, In the Good Old Summertime, The Barkleys of Broadway, The Great Sinner and Greer Garson in That Forsyte Woman.

SLAUGHTER ON TENTH AVENUE
A Universal-International Picture (1957)

Directed by Arnold Laven. Produced by Albert Zugsmith. Based on the book "The Man Who Rocked the Boat" by William J. Keating and Richard Carter. Photography by Fred Jackman. Costumes by Bill Thomas. Edited by Russell F. Schoengarth. Running time, 103 minutes.
CAST: William Keating, RICHARD EGAN; Madge Pitts, JAN STERLING; Dee, JULIE ADAMS; John Jacob Masters, DAN DURYEA; Al Dahlke, WALTER MATTHAU; Lt. Anthony Vosnick, CHARLES McGRAW; Howard Rysdale, SAM LEVENE. Guest Star, HEDY LAMARR.
NOTE: Miss Lamarr's cameo appearance in this feature film was deleted before the movie was released.

With Julie Adams in the scene cut from SLAUGHTER ON TENTH AVENUE

THE LOVE GODDESSES
A Walter Reade–Sterling Picture (1964)
A Saul J. Turell–Graeme Ferguson Production

Produced and written by Saul J. Turell *and* Graeme Ferguson. *Narrated by* Carl King. *Music by* Percy Faith. *Edited by* Nat Greene *and* Howard Kuperman. *Running time, 87 minutes. A compilation of film clips whom the producers of this project believed to be the screen's great love "goddesses." Hedy Lamarr is seen romping through her famous* Ecstasy; *Lya De Putti in* The Sorrows of Satan; *Clara Bow, Hula; Mae West, I'm No Angel; Rita Hayworth, Gilda; Betty Grable, College Swing; Marilyn Monroe, Some Like It Hot; Marlene Dietrich, Blonde Venus and Morocco; and Dorothy Lamour, Jean Harlow, Theda Bara, Pola Negri, Louise Glaum, Lana Turner, Sophia Loren, Greta Garbo, Elizabeth Taylor, Brigitte Bardot and Carole Lombard to name a few. Included were such stars who could hardly be qualified as Love Goddesses—Bette Davis! Jeannette MacDonald! Shirley Temple! and Ruby Keeler!*

THAT'S ENTERTAINMENT, 2
United Artists (1976)

Filmed in Panavision and Metrocolor. New sequences directed by Gene Kelly. Produced by Saul Chaplin and David Melnick. Music arranged and conducted by Nelson Riddle. Narration written by Leonard Gershe. Photography by George Folsey. Production designed by John De Cuir. Sound by Bill Edmondson. Edited by Bud Friedgen and David Blewitt. Running time, 126 minutes.

Hedy Lamarr is seen in a closeup delivering her famous "I am Tondeleyo" line from White Cargo. *Highlights of the 66 musical numbers included "Have Yourself a Merry Little Christmas" (Judy Garland and Margaret O'Brien, Meet Me in St. Louis); "Hi-Lili, Hi-Lo" (Leslie Caron, Lili); "The Lady is a Tramp" (Lena Horne, Words and Music); 'Ten Cents a Dance' (Doris Day, Love Me or Leave Me); "The Last Time I Saw Paris" (Dinah Shore, Till the Clouds Roll By); "Easter Parade" (Fred Astaire and Judy Garland, Easter Parade); "There's No Business Like Show Business" (Betty Hutton, Annie Get Your Gun). Katharine Hepburn, Spencer Tracy, Greer Garson, Clark Gable and Vivien Leigh were just a few stars seen in non-musical clips.*

Georgi Gragore

THE LAMARR WOMEN

Eva

Gaby

Karen Vanmeer

Manon de Vargnes

Marvin Myles

Sandra Kolter

Theodore

Johanna "Johnny" Jones

Lucienne Talbot
Tondelayo

Vicky Whitley
Dolores "Sweets" Ramirez

Irene von Mohr

Allida Bederaux

Princess Veronica

Madeleine Damien

Jenny Hager (Opposite page)

Dr. Loring

Delilah

Marianne Lorress

Lisa Roselle

Lily Dalbray

La Eterna Femmina

Joan of Arc

Vanessa Windsor

HEDY ON TELEVISION

TOAST OF THE TOWN
CBS-TV

September 17, 1950   8:00 P.M.   60 minutes

Host/ED SULLIVAN
Guest Stars/HEDY LAMARR, PAT O'BRIEN and MIMI BENZELL.

THE COLGATE COMEDY HOUR
NBC-TV

May 11, 1952   8:00 P.M.   60 minutes

A variety show combining comedy and music and starring DONALD O'CONNOR.

Guest Stars/HEDY LAMARR, ANTHONY DEXTER (the actor who starred in *VALENTINO* and MARTHA TILTON.

ALL-STAR REVIEW
NBC-TV

June 14, 1952   8:00 P.M.   60 minutes

A variety series of comedy and music with comedians rotating each week as the headliner. This program was in the capable hands of PAUL WINCHELL with his dummy JERRY MAHONEY. HEDY LAMARR was the very attractive guest star.

THE COLGATE COMEDY HOUR
NBC-TV

December 28, 1952   8:00 P.M.   60 minutes

Star-Host/BEN BLUE
Guest Stars/HEDY LAMARR, PEGGY LEE, PHIL HARRIS, and THE SPORTSMEN.

MISS LAMARR appeared with BLUE in a sketch about the wild goings-on among spies at the Hotel Intrigue.

Rehearsing TOAST OF THE TOWN with Ed Sullivan

With Donald O'Connor on THE COLGATE COMEDY HOUR

With Jack Benny on SHOWER OF STARS

THE COLGATE COMEDY HOUR
NBC-TV

March 8, 1953   8:00 P.M.   60 minutes

DONALD O'CONNOR, again the star of this show, sang and danced around the Manhattan skyline. And in a spoof, opera becomes the bop-era.

Guest Stars/HEDY LAMARR, CECIL KELLAWAY, HAL MARCH, SID MILLER *and* TOM D'ANDREA.

SHOWER OF STARS
CBS-TV

March 14, 1957   8:30 P.M.   60 minutes

Star/JACK BENNY

Guest Stars/HEDY LAMARR, GALE STORM, JACQUES d'AMBOISE, LAWRENCE WELK *and* SID KROFFT.

A variety show in which all the guests joined BENNY in a sketch take-off on cloak-and-dagger dramas set in an international casino. A dance number featured d'AMBOISE and a three-foot marionette handled by KROFFT.

THE PERRY COMO SHOW
NBC-TV

March 30, 1957   8:00 P.M.   60 minutes

Guest Stars/HEDY LAMARR, JULIUS LA ROSA *and* DAN ROWAN & DICK MARTIN.

In this show, which had a Springtime theme, PERRY COMO sang "April in Paris," "Round and Round" and "Hi, Neighbor."

I'VE GOT A SECRET
CBS-TV

April 10, 1957   9:30 P.M.   30 minutes

Host/GARRY MOORE
Guest Star/HEDY LAMARR
Panelists/FAYE EMERSON, JAYNE MEADOWS, HENRY MORGAN and BILL CULLEN

A game show on which the panelists tried to guess the secret of the weekly guest celebrity.

THE GEORGE GOBEL SHOW
NBC-TV

October 22, 1957   8:00 P.M.   60 minutes

Star/GEORGE GOBEL
Guest Stars/HEDY LAMARR, EDDIE FISHER, SHIRLEY HAMER, BARBARA BOSTOCK, HOWARD McNEAR and JOHN SCOTT TROTTER and the Orchestra. With THE JOHNNY MANN SINGERS.

The show's theme /"Glamour Through the Ages." In a comedy sketch, GEORGE GOBEL brings his dogs into a poodle parlor presided over by HEDY LAMARR.

With George Gobel on THE GEORGE GOBEL SHOW

With Roy Roberts on the ZANE GREY THEATRE

ZANE GREY THEATRE
PROUD WOMAN
CBS-TV

October 25, 1957   8:30 P.M.   30 minutes

Host/DICK POWELL

CAST

Consuela Bowers, HEDY LAMARR; *Frank Fayne*, PAUL RICHARDS; *Michael Bowers*, ROY ROBERTS; *Esteban*, EDWARD COLMANS; *Maria Delgado*, IPHIGENIE CASTIGLIONI

PLOT

When Consuela Bowers arrives in the West, she hires a man to work on her father's ranch. She does not know that he is a professional gunman involved in a plot to steal a valuable horse.

THE TONIGHT SHOW
NBC-TV

April 23, 1962   11:15 P.M.   95 minutes

Host/ROBERT CUMMINGS
Guest Stars/HEDY LAMARR, JAYNE MANSFIELD, VINCENT PRICE, PATRICIA MORISON and MOULTON TAYLOR and his flying automobile.

STUMP THE STARS
CBS-TV

November 19, 1962   10:30 P.M.   30 minutes

Host/PAT HARRINGTON, JR.

HEDY LAMARR joined the team of JAN CLAYTON, SEBASTIAN CABOT and ROSS MARTIN on this game show to play charades against BEVERLY GARLAND, BARBARA NICHOLS, RICARDO MONTALBAN and MICKEY MANNERS.

Playing charades with Jan Clayton, Sebastian Cabot and Ross Martin on STUMP THE STARS

CELEBRITY GAME
CBS-TV

May 3, 1964   9:00 P.M.   30 minutes

Moderator/CARL REINER
Celebrity Panelists/HEDY LAMARR, WALTER BRENNAN, JOSEPH COTTEN, BETTY HUTTON, EDD BYRNES, EARTHA KITT, PAUL LYNDE, CLIFF ARQUETTE and SHERI LEWIS

Dancing with Jimmy O'Neil on SHINDIG

CELEBRITY GAME
CBS-TV

September 6, 1964   9:00 P.M.   30 minutes

Celebrity Panelists/HEDY LAMARR, TOM TRYON, DIANE McBAIN, JOSEPH COTTEN, DELLA REESE, BETTY HUTTON, PAUL LYNDE, RAY WALSTON and ANDY DEVINE.

SHINDIG
ABC-TV

October 21, 1965   7:30 P.M.   30 minutes

Host/JIMMY O'NEIL
Guests/HEDY LAMARR, THE DAVE CLARK FIVE, THE KINGSMEN, BRENDA HOLLOWAY, JOE TEX, THE BLOSSOMS, THE ELIGIBLES and EDDIE RAMBEAU performing music of the rock-pop era.

BOB HOPE COMEDY SPECIAL
NBC-TV

September 28, 1966   9:00 P.M.   60 minutes

Starring *BOB HOPE* and his *LEADING LADIES:* HEDY LAMARR, DOROTHY LAMOUR, LUCILLE BALL, JOAN FONTAINE, JOAN COLLINS, MARILYN MAXWELL, VIRGINIA MAYO, VERA MILES, JOAN CAULFIELD, ARLENE DAHL, RHONDA FLEMING, DINA MERRILL, SIGNE HASSO, JANIS PAIGE and PHYLLIS DILLER. Also Starring: JERRY COLONNA, PAUL LYNDE, KEN MURRAY and LES BROWN and HIS BAND OF RENOWN.

THE DICK CAVETT SHOW
ABC-TV

June 2, 1969   10:00 P.M.   60 minutes

A one-hour variety-talk show hosted by DICK CAVETT. Guests/HEDY LAMARR, REX REED and NICOL WILLIAMSON.

THE MIKE DOUGLAS SHOW
CBS-TV

August 12, 1969   4:30 P.M.   90 minutes
(New York City)

Other dates in different areas.
Host/MIKE DOUGLAS
Guests/HEDY LAMARR, REX REED, FRANKIE VALLI, TINY TIM and NORM CROSBY.

THE DAVID FROST SHOW
Westinghouse Broadcasting

August 14, 1969   8:30 P.M.   90 minutes
(New York City)

Other dates in different areas.
Host/DAVID FROST
Guests/HEDY LAMARR, comedian PAT HENRY, and the singing PRIMO FAMILY.

Opposite page (below) BOB HOPE COMEDY SPECIAL—Front row, left to right: Lucille Ball, Joan Fontaine, Hedy and Signe Hasso.
Back row, left to right: Joan Collins, Dorothy Lamour, Hope, Virginia Mayo, Vera Miles and Janis Paige

With Merv Griffin on THE MERV GRIFFIN SHOW

PERSONALITY
NBC-TV

August 15, 1969   11:00 A.M.   30 minutes

On film/HEDY LAMARR
Game Celebrities/RITA MORENO, TOM KENNEDY and ROCKY GRAZIANO

THE MERV GRIFFIN SHOW
CBS-TV

August 18, 1969   11:30 P.M.   90 minutes

Host/MERV GRIFFIN
Guests/HEDY LAMARR, WOODY ALLEN, LESLIE UGGAMS and JACKIE "MOMS" MABLEY.

With Mike Douglas, Norm Crosby, Rex Reed and Tiny Tim on THE MIKE DOUGLAS SHOW

Entertaining G.I.s at the Hollywood Canteen during World War II

LIFE GOES TO WAR
NBC-TV

September 18, 1977   9:00 P.M.   2 hours

Host/JOHNNY CARSON

Clips from the bombing of Pearl Harbor, General MacArthur's celebrated return to the Philippines, and on the home front—scenes of rationing, scrap drives and civil-defense drills. One of the themes is Hollywood's role in the war effort. HEDY LAMARR is shown on bond tours and entertaining at the Hollywood Canteen. Other stars are seen in U.S.O. shows and opening their homes to G.I.'s.

NBC:
THE FIRST FIFTY YEARS
– A CLOSER LOOK
NBC-TV

October 23, 1977   8:30 P.M.   2¹/₂ hours

Host-Narrator/ORSON WELLES
Guest Hosts/CHEVY CHASE, GEORGE BURNS, BURT REYNOLDS, DAN HAGGERTY and DON RICKLES.

A half century of musical and comedy moments from many of NBC's memorable programs. HEDY LAMARR was shown from her guest appearance on THE PERRY COMO SHOW in 1957.

NOTE

MISS LAMARR also appeared on THE ARTHUR MURRAY DANCE PARTY, and with her children DENISE and TONY on TO TELL THE TRUTH. Airing dates for these programs could not be located.